D1796783

The Phillip Island
MURDER
The true account of a
brutal killing

Vikki Petraitis and Paul Daley

PENNON
PUBLISHING
2004

First published in Australia in 1994
This edition published in 2004 by
Pennon Publishing
59 Fletcher Street
Essendon Vic 3041
www.pennon.com.au

Text copyright © Vikki Petraitis and Paul Daley

All rights reserved. No part of this book may be reproduced, stored in a
retrieval system, or transmitted in any form or by any means electronic,
mechanical or otherwise, without the prior written permission of the
publisher.

Every effort has been made to ensure that this book is free from error or
omissions. However, the publisher, the author and their respective employees
or agents, do not accept responsibility for injury, loss or damage occasioned
to any person acting or refraining from action as a result of material in this
book whether or not such injury, loss or damage is in any way due to any
negligent act or omission, breach of duty or default on the part of the
publisher, the author, or their respective employees or agents.

The National Library of Australia
Cataloguing-in-Publication entry:

Petraitis, Vikki, 1965-
        The Phillip Island murder.

        ISBN 1 877029 81 5.

        1. Barnard, Beth. 2. Cameron, Vivienne. 3. Murder -
        Victoria - Phillip Island. 4. Missing persons -
        Investigation - Victoria - Phillip Island. 5. Murder
        victims - Victoria - Phillip Island. I. Daley, Paul. II.
        Title.

        364.1523099452

Designed by Allan Cornwell
Printed in Australia by The Craftsman Press

CONTENTS

ABOUT THE AUTHORS

VIKKI PETRAITIS WAS BORN AND BROUGHT UP IN MELBOURNE. She teaches in a suburban primary school. She began researching this book in July 1991.

Paul Daley grew up in Melbourne and graduated from the University of Melbourne in 1987. He wrote for a number of Melbourne newspapers until the first publication of the *Sunday Age* in 1989, where he works as an investigative reporter and senior features writer. This is his second book.

ACKNOWLEDGEMENTS

MANY PEOPLE HELPED WITH THIS BOOK, too many to thank all of them. However, there are some who deserve special mention. The authors would like to extend their gratitude to the many people close to the victim, Beth Barnard, who chose to talk about their friend. For sharing their memories, some of them painful, we thank them. Thank you, also, to all those friends of Vivienne Cameron who shared their memories of a woman who, by all accounts, was a loving mother and a solid friend.

Thanks to all members of the Victoria Police who generously gave their time to assist in the reconstruction of the murder investigation and helped ensure the accuracy of this book. While a number of police took a special interest in this book, special acknowledgement must go to Senior Constable Rory O'Connor, formerly of the Homicide Squad; Senior Constable Brian Gamble of the State Forensic Science Laboratory; Detective Jack McFayden of Wonthaggi Criminal Investigation Branch; Sergeant Geoff Frost of the Victoria Police Search and Rescue Squad; and Senior Constable Michael Barry.

The authors also thank the staff of Coronial Services in Melbourne who made themselves available for interview: State Coroner Hal Hallenstein, Dr David Ranson, Dr Bentley Atchison, David Stevens and Magdelene Dratsas.

All reconstructions in this book are based on extensive interviews, and police and Coronial statements taken from witnesses about the time of the tragedy.

Some names in this book have been changed to protect anonymity.

INTRODUCTION

THE ORIGIN OF THIS BOOK LIES WITH VIKKI PETRAITIS and her fascination with, first, crime fiction, then, increasingly, crime non-fiction in her reading. She first heard of the death of Beth Barnard and the disappearance of Vivienne Cameron from the newspaper reports of the investigation. Some time later she was on Phillip Island by happenstance and the talk of the Islanders about the case began to exercise some fascination within her. She did a bit of digging and fascination soon turned into a growing horror at what appeared to be the setting into action of a course of events that was to result in the deaths of two women and leave scars elsewhere.

Then research – obtaining documents, cataloguing, analysis, comparison, interviews, footwork, and cross checking information – began in earnest. Vikki Petraitis was to accumulate many shelf-metres of material before Paul Daley was approached to co-operate on the venture. The first result was a whole lot more research, as new avenues to the understanding of this crime were opened up and investigated.

One of the aims of the book became to present the reader with the true nature of a major homicide investigation, the limits and capabilities of forensic work, the footwork, the many fruitless leads that have to be followed up, and all the detail involved. This book explains how the investigation worked. It makes no claim to provide a definitive account of what exactly happened on the night of 22 September 1986. Possibly someone died that night, taking the knowledge with them.

The authors can state some things did happen, and other things did not, or could not, have happened. The most detailed, exhaustive analysis by police and the authors' own work on the case leave problems unsolved or insoluble. A court, working on probabilities from detailed evidence, has ruled that a woman, motivated by jealousy, killed another and jumped to her death.

Vikki Petraitis
Paul Daley
Melbourne, 1993

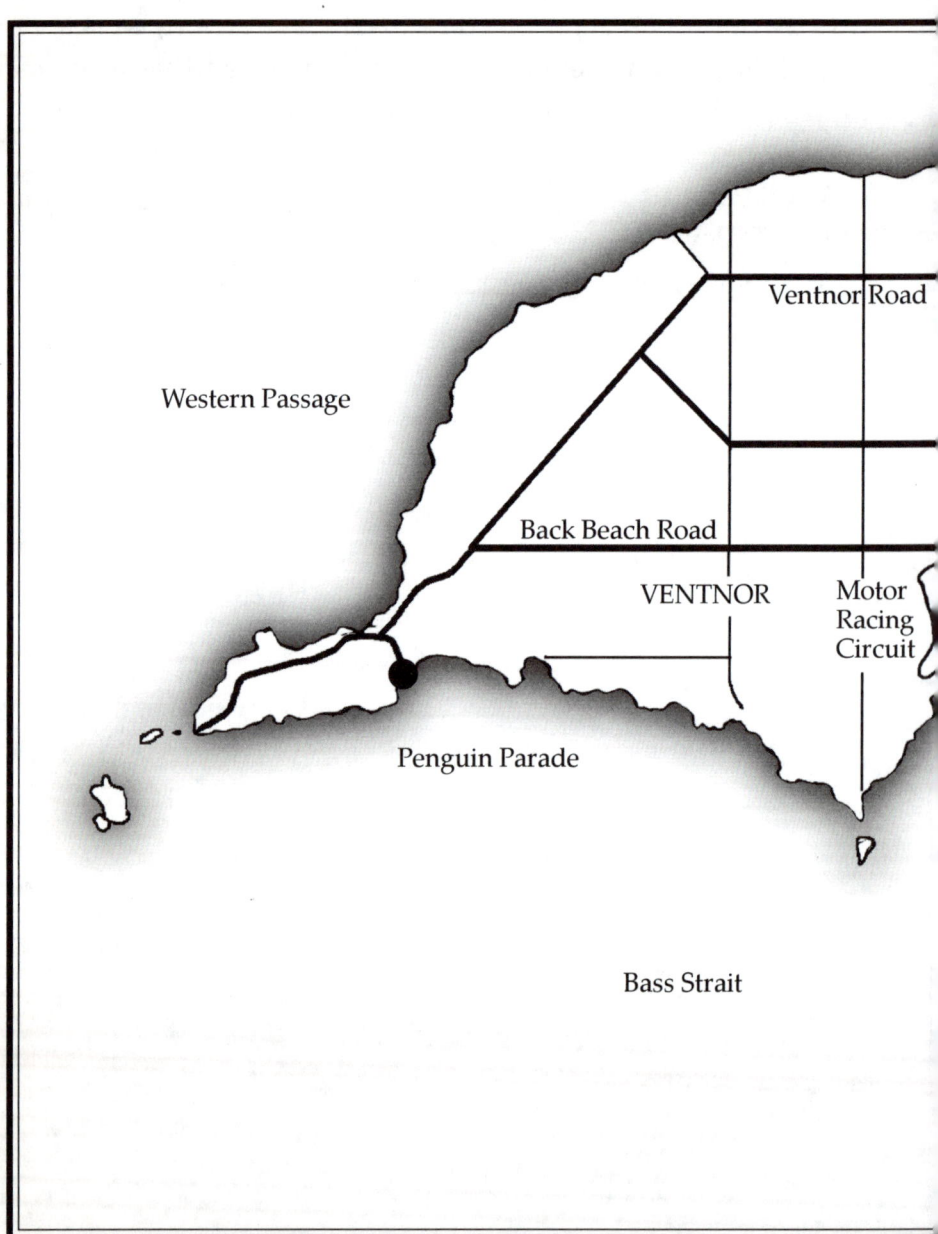

Ventnor Road

Western Passage

Back Beach Road

VENTNOR

Motor
Racing
Circuit

Penguin Parade

Bass Strait

WES

RHYLL

N
W   E
S

1   0   1   2   3

McFees Road

Phillip Island Road

NEWHAVEN

SAN REMO
To Melbourne →

Eastern Passage

Chapter One
A Body Find

PHILLIP ISLAND IS THE PERFECT PLACE FOR AN AGEING POLICE OFFICER TO FINISH HIS PROFESSIONAL DAYS.

Compared with the string of city stations and the vice squad where Sergeant Cliff Ashe had worked during his 29 years in the force, 'The Island' – as the locals call it – is a peaceful backwater. Phillip Island is, for the most part, a pleasant holiday resort with a wealth of unusual attractions, including a penguin parade, a koala reserve and a Grand Prix Race Track – all packed into the relatively small area of 10,105 hectares.

The main body of Phillip Island is weathered volcanic rock; a natural phenomenon that gives rise to an incredibly diverse 90 kilometres of coastline including 46 kilometres of beaches perfectly suited to sheltered swimming.

These safe swimming areas are, however, in direct contrast with the extremely dangerous rocky cliffs at the most south-western point of the island. The rugged coastline includes a jagged, craggy conglomeration known as The Nobbies, and the tumultuous Blowhole at Point Grant where huge white-capped waves crash into each other shooting the ensuing spray high into the air.

The 4000 full-time residents of Phillip Island are mostly employed in farming, fishing, recreation and small businesses – recreational activities are especially important to the economy of the island, which relies on summer holiday-makers each year injecting millions of dollars into local coffers. The greater proportion of many beach resort areas on Phillip Island are mostly comprised of holiday homes that are occasionally inhabited on weekends during the colder months and, often, full-time during summer.

Crime on the island is usually confined to the occasional break-in of a weekend tourist's house, the odd car accident and drink-driving case or, during the summer when thousands of holiday-makers swarm there for the sun, surf and easy living, police are sometimes required to attend a swimming accident at one of the treacherous surf beaches. The Island is also, quite literally, a favoured location for those wanting to end their days in solace. Disillusioned people frequently jump to their deaths – usually from a rugged cliff-face on the far south of the island, The Nobbies – into dangerous waters surrounding Phillip Island. Their remains are rarely found intact, because these seas are a favoured breeding ground for sea lice and a variety of ferocious sharks.

There is also the occasional wild brawl at Phillip Island's only hotel, the Isle of Wight. But even then, the local police usually aren't too fazed because, just across a bridge joining the island to mainland Victoria is the township of San Remo and another police station where reinforcements can quickly be gathered.

Ironically for one of Victoria's most peaceful and law-abiding hamlets, Cowes – Phillip Island's township – becomes one of the busiest policing areas in the state on 31 December each year, when thousands of drunks gather to count down the final seconds of the year. The locked door of an overcrowded cell and a court summons for drunk and disorderly behaviour are all the New Year holds for many such visitors to The Island.

There's a certain pride which only country policing can bring and Cliff Ashe found his in knowing that, while he'd been in charge of the island, it was famous for its penguins – which each night cross the beach in their hundreds to reach their burrows in the sand dunes – not its crime rate. Like other local police, he expected there might be some trouble in a couple of years when the Australian leg of the world Formula One Motorcycle Grand Prix was held there. But force command in Melbourne, 110 kilometres away, could anticipate that.

Ashe, a tall, greying man who carried a typical air of the tough but fair, no nonsense cop, had more pressing concerns on Tuesday 23 September 1986. On his first day back after annual leave, a bulging file of paperwork waited on his desk in the small, dilapidated Cowes Police Station. It was appropriate the National Trust intended to preserve the building, though the police, who daily had to endure its obsolescence, would thankfully soon be moving shop into a new brick building next door.

No sooner had Ashe thrown himself into the station's tedious, albeit pressing, administrative duties, than two of the island's most prominent residents closed the wire door behind them. Like many of the 4000 people who lived in his policing territory, Ashe knew the names of these men – another hallmark, but sometimes a disadvantage, of being a country cop. Preoccupied by his paperwork, Ashe didn't address them by name. They were Ian Cairns and Donald Cameron, brothers-in-law.

'How can I help you gentlemen?'

'There's been a domestic argument...' muttered Cameron, who was well-known because of his membership of the local council and for having forged a reputation for being outspoken and direct, never meek or lost for a word. Today, however, Donald Cameron couldn't seem to get to the point. He talked on, apparently unaware that Sergeant Ashe was busy. So why, wondered Cliff Ashe, have I listened to this diatribe, to Don Cameron's vague ramblings for the past 10 minutes about family fights and family conferences, about Cameron's brother Fergus and his secret affair with a young female farmhand on his property, Beth Barnard?

'Donald,' Ashe interrupted, 'exactly what are you trying to tell me?'

'Um, it's Beth,' he said, leaning over the counter even further and looking from side to side. 'I think she's not well.' Donald Cameron, the man famous for speaking his mind, had just become the master of understatement.

At the weekend farmhouse of her Queen's Counsellor father in McFees Road, Ryhll – about 10 minutes' drive from the police station – 23-year-old Beth Barnard was, indeed, 'not well' at all.

She was dead. And Donald Cameron knew it.

'We were just at her place and she was lying on the floor with blood everywhere,' Cameron said.

Ashe immediately placed a call to the Wonthaggi Police Station and requested that the Criminal Investigation Branch detectives meet him at McFees Road, Rhyll – a possible murder scene. Ten minutes later Cameron and Cairns pulled their car into the driveway of a colonial-style brick farmhouse. Right behind them in the police car was Ashe and one of his juniors from the station, Senior Constable Peter McHenry. Ashe knew too well, after attending 'body finds' so many times in Melbourne, that the first thing he should do was 'preserve' the crime scene to make sure any evidence wasn't tampered with. He also knew the detectives he'd called from Wonthaggi would be at the farmhouse shortly and – thinking it was possible or even probable, given their vague complaint, that Cameron and Cairns had made a mistake – he wanted to make sure the person in the house really was dead. What if she's in there bleeding to death and I'm out here guarding the house? he thought.

As he walked toward the back of the house Ashe noticed that both the screen door and the wooden door were unlocked and slightly ajar. He knew straight away that if somebody had attacked the woman inside they had no trouble getting in... probably even knew her.

Three steps inside the door brought him to the bedroom where Elizabeth Barnard, or Beth as she was known, usually slept. She lay on the floor, her head toward the door where Ashe stood staring, her bright, blue eyes fixed on the ceiling. A quilt covered her from the nose down and, while the pool of congealed blood on the carpet around her head made it obvious to Ashe she was dead, he could see no injuries.

Ashe pinched a corner of the quilt and carefully peeled it away from her nose, revealing a horror he'd never forget: her throat had been cut to the neck bone like that of a slaughterhouse animal and a savage knife blow had sliced through her top lip, smashing out a top front tooth. Ashe was relieved to place the quilt back over Beth's mouth before he slowly left the room, shaking his head, to re-enter the bright sunny day and the welcome fresh air outside. There he was soon met by the Wonthaggi detectives – Sergeant Ron Cooper, Senior Constable Alan McFayden [known affectionately to his colleagues as 'Jack'] and Senior Detective Alan Lowe. Ashe contacted the Homicide Squad in Melbourne by his car radio and then moved the police car out of the driveway, while the detectives cordoned off the house with blue and white tape, indicating that it had become a 'crime scene'. The property would be thoroughly checked for evidence and the driveway would later be checked for tyre marks.

Senior Constable Jack McFayden was a big man with hair greying at the edges and a handshake like a vice. Like Ashe, he'd seen countless bodies during his time with the Victoria Police. But scenes like this disturbed him nonetheless. He entered the farmhouse and looked down at the dead woman. He shook his head sadly. It was so senseless, he thought. A pretty girl who had probably been planning her future, experimenting with life and excited about what lay ahead. Butchered. No future now, just a statistic. All plans laid to rest.

Dreadful, thought McFayden, that in death – particularly when it happens like this – there's no privacy, no dignity. Soon other men she would never have met will come traipsing through her room to look through her letters and record the numbers in her telephone directory, stare at her mutilated body, search through her underwear drawers and diaries and expose her secrets. He knew that murder precluded a victim's privacy and Beth's life was now an open book to investigators. Her death, like the records of her life, had become their property.

He noticed that the bedroom curtains were fully drawn and in stark contrast with the spring brightness outside, a dim light from a bedside lamp cast deep shadows across the bedroom. There were two single beds and the usual mess – jeans, underwear, jumpers and shoes – dropped by an active, carefree woman. There were photographs of Beth, her sister and her parents, and her chest of drawers was cluttered with perfume and cosmetic bottles, more photos and two stuffed toy animals. A bottle of cough medicine and some cold and flu tablets, some light pain-relief tablets and a glass of water were also on top of the drawers.

One of the stuffed toy animals was a penguin – testimony to the many hours Beth had worked part time at the Phillip Island Penguin Parade, when she wasn't working on the farm of Donald Cameron's brother – and her lover, Fergus.

Only metres from the dead woman under the quilt, a blown-up photograph, mounted on board, leaned upright against one of the beds. Beth, tall, strong and attractive, smiled broadly as she held two baby penguins. Now her blood was splattered across her jeans and a pair of old sneakers on the floor. Her formal black dress hung neatly on a coat hanger from the door and her battered Akubra hat sat on a bedpost.

Beth's head was just inside the doorway and McFayden too, lifted the quilt to see the sickening gashes on her throat and mouth. He checked the rest of the house to see if there were any more bodies or indeed, if the killer was hiding in another room. As he joined the growing group of police and onlookers outside, McFayden heard a detective say: 'Whoever did this didn't leave unscathed.' They were referring to droplets of blood, forming a meagre trail, on the path leading away from the back door.

McFayden left soon afterwards for the police station with Ian Cairns and Donald Cameron, where he would take their statements. About the same time, Senior Constable Peter McHenry went to the Newhaven Medical Centre to collect the local doctor, Paul Flood – only a few days earlier Beth had gone to him complaining of a cold.

But before he'd see the bloodied body under the quilt – which he wouldn't automatically recognise as Beth – Dr Flood would go to the home of Ian Cairns in Ventnor, where he'd examine the man who'd last seen Beth – Fergus Cameron.

While Dr Flood was on his way to see Fergus, homicide squad detectives Rory O'Connor and Garry Hunter arrived at the Barnard house. They in turn had organised crime scene officers and a police photographer and fingerprint experts to attend the house in McFees Road as soon as possible.

O'Connor, a handsome detective in his late thirties whose hair was on the cusp of silver, quickly learnt a few details about the killing from Donald Cameron.

He listened carefully: last night Fergus Cameron's wife had attacked him when he admitted having an affair with the dead woman and, according to Donald Cameron, the wife, Vivienne, had stabbed Fergus with a broken wineglass and taken him to the hospital for stitches. Donald said Vivienne had then dropped Fergus at the home of his sister, Marnie, who was married to Ian Cairns, where he had stayed the night.

Donald said Vivienne had then arranged for somebody to mind her two young boys before she drove a short way to the Barnard's house. She may then have murdered Beth. Although family members had checked her home, they had failed to locate Vivienne Cameron or her family's Toyota Land Cruiser.

Sounds simple enough, thought O'Connor. He knew it was imperative that Vivienne be found, but just as importantly, he tried not to reach hasty conclusions about the missing woman. She was, however, a key suspect.

O'Connor's quick calculation put Fergus Cameron near the top of the list too.

He and Detective Hunter had been warned before they went into the house about the horrific damage to Beth's face and throat. But nothing could prepare them for what they saw when O'Connor lifted the quilt off her semi-naked body.

They couldn't help but stare at a huge symbol that had been

carved into Beth's chest, extending to her abdomen.

Hunter and O'Connor stared, trying to make sense of the slashes that had cut through Beth's chest and stomach muscles down to the ribs.

It was the letter 'A'.

Chapter Two

A Doomed Struggle

SOME THINGS ABOUT BETH BARNARD'S DEATH ARE ABSOLUTELY CERTAIN. THE FORENSIC PATHOLOGISTS HAVE LITTLE DOUBT ABOUT THE ORDER IN WHICH THE WOUNDS TO BETH'S BODY WERE MADE, AND FROM THE FIRST CUT TO THE LAST, THE KILLER'S PROGRESS THROUGH THE HOUSE SEEMS TO BE FAIRLY WELL ESTABLISHED.

What remains uncertain to this day, however – and the question that appears unlikely to ever be resolved with absolute certainty – is the identity and whereabouts of her killer or killers.

The murder scene was lit by the back-porch light and the police assume the bedside lamp had illuminated the sleeping woman because it was still switched on when the body was discovered. Because of the heavy bloodstains on the bedclothes under which Beth had been sleeping, and because of a bloodied hand print on the wall near the bed, detectives are almost certain that the attack began with Beth asleep or, at least, in her bed.

It seems unlikely that the killer was unfamiliar with the house and its layout of rooms, although a complete stranger can never be ruled out fully as the perpetrator.

The back porch light shone against the darkness of the back of the farmhouse and a figure stood in the unlit hallway. Three bedroom doors were visible to the intruder from the hallway and a short step was all it took to enter Beth's bedroom.

The intruder walked over to Beth's single bed and turned on the bedside lamp which dimly illuminated ornaments on a chest of drawers next to the sleeping woman. The intruder raised the knife, aimed for Beth's chest and brought it crashing down, making a crunching noise as metal struck flesh and bone. The knife disappeared to the hilt.

Beth was jolted awake. Her hand clutched at the knife in her chest and her stunned eyes probably met those of her killer. She grabbed at the blade and it sliced painfully into her right hand as it was extracted from her body. She flung her hand to the wall by her bed leaving a bloodied impression, and scrambled onto all fours on the bed in a vain attempt to escape from what she had probably realised was a deadly attack. Her killer began flailing wildly with the blood-covered knife as Beth rolled off the bed and landed at the murderer's feet, again presenting herself as a perfect target for another agonising blow.

The fatal wound skewered her chest just below the right collar bone at once puncturing Beth's right lung, which began immediately to fill with blood. Beth raised her arms above her chest to ward off the deadly, persistent blows. The next thrust caught her deep in the elbow. Beth kicked at her killer, who jammed the knife down into her left ankle, splashing blood onto the white chest of drawers beside where she lay struggling for her life.

At some stage it is likely that a farm dog that usually slept in the laundry came into the room, barking. The dog – protective of Beth – may have jumped at the killer, who would have been forced to grab the dog's collar and run with it to the back door.

The killer would then have shut the back door and returned to the bedroom. Beth may have managed to kick her killer off balance, buying time to roll over and crawl toward the door. There is no doubt she tried to escape the killer, but her breathing was becoming laboured and she rolled onto her back and gasped for breath. She still managed to pull herself into a sitting position causing the blood to flow freely from her chest, down her stomach and onto her blue and white striped underpants. The killer walked towards her and again slashed out suddenly with the knife.

As the blade struck her again, Beth desperately held up her hand to catch another blow and the knife sliced deeply between her thumb and forefinger. At this point Beth probably opened her mouth to scream just as the next knife blow caught her face with such force it sliced her upper lip in half and knocked out her left front tooth which landed on the carpet by her side. The pain would have been indescribable.

Judging from the injuries, the murderer took up a position behind the woman who, besides her gasps, was probably quiet and exhausted. Her bleeding hands grasped at her thighs, leaving smeared bloody impressions. Her body heaved in its battle for oxygen and slowly faded from consciousness.

The murderer held Beth's head tightly, twisting it violently to the left. She was now completely powerless in the hands of a murderer ready for the coup de grace.

The knife slashed quickly and deliberately across Beth's throat. Instinctively, she tried to move her head to stop the knife slicing into her neck, but by now the arm holding her head was too strong. After the first two slashes, Beth probably stopped struggling.

The murderer slashed until Beth's head began to come away from her body. Beth's battered, bleeding form hit the carpet with a thud as the murderer let go and blood flowed freely from her throat, her blue eyes staring vacantly at the ceiling – nothing more could be done to hurt her now. The killer stepped back and looked at the results of the death fight. It would have taken no longer than a couple of minutes from beginning to end.

She was dead. The killer walked from the bedroom into the hallway and probably paused and took a deep breath.

But there were still things to be done.

The killer entered the bathroom knowing that this part was as important as the murder itself. Blood-soaked hands reached out and twisted on the bathroom taps and the water came out in a rush. Blood and water dripped on to the porcelain around the taps and the hands wrung together to remove the red smears. Flicking blood-soaked hands towards the bath, the killer left red droplets against the white surface.

Because a cigarette butt was found in an ashtray in the bathroom, police believe the killer then smoked a cigarette, flicking ash into a clean ash tray on the vanity unit. The cigarette burned until only the brand name, Peter Stuyvesant, was visible before it was extinguished. It was now time to return to the body.

The killer looked at Beth's remains, took up the knife which had extinguished her life, and touched it to the cooling flesh of her chest. The killer had an idea: the death must look appropriate, and so the incision began at the breast bone and carved deeply into the chest, diagonally down towards the hip. Once the killer judged the length to be right, the knife stopped and returned to the breast bone again. This time the incision went diagonally the other way, creating an inverted 'V'. The killer reviewed the handiwork and carved more deeply on the left side, peeling the skin open to expose the yellow fatty tissue underneath. The killer didn't continue this, but moved toward completing the design.

A short bar was cut just above the navel to complete the letter 'A' over the torso. The wooden-handled, bloodstained knife was placed on the carpet next to the body.

The killer's work was almost done. But there was one last thing – the body must be covered.

A quilt was taken from a single bed in the next bedroom, brought into Beth's blood-splattered room and carefully placed over her body so that only the top of her head was showing. It was still obvious she was dead because of her open, staring eyes and the blood congealing beneath her head on the carpet. But no wounds were visible.

The path to the back door was short, and the killer disappeared quickly in a waiting vehicle into the night.

What the forensic science experts can't tell us are what words and sounds filled that small bedroom on the night of Beth Barnard's death. Beyond certainty, however, there were gasps for breath and liquid gurgles in a lung mortally opened up by a deadly knife, the silence of a woman rendered mute by the gashes to her mouth and throat at the end of the attack, and the barks and whines of the distressed dog.

Did she have time to ask why? It is more than likely that Beth knew her attacker, because there was no sign of forced entry into the house that was always securely locked. Was Beth awake before the attack began? If the initial attack happened while she was in her bed, was she entertaining a guest? We can be fairly certain that she screamed and protested because of the injuries she sustained while fighting and defending herself.

Another gruesome possibility, later suggested by a police crime scene officer, is that the killer rubbed his or her bloodied hands all over Beth's arms, legs and torso causing extensive blood smears – more than would have occurred incidentally in the attack.

Forensic evidence tells us something about the manner of the killer. The killer was strong. The stabs and lunges suggest absolute commitment to killing Beth from the first blow, and probably before entry into the dark farmhouse. But even the time of death was never definitely established, and the evidence does not tell us who it was, or why.

Chapter Three

Sun, Sand, Problems, Plans

DURING HER TIME AT THE PENGUIN PARADE, AND THROUGHOUT THE YEARS THAT BETH'S PARENTS HAD OWNED THEIR WEEKEND HOUSE ON PHILLIP ISLAND, BETH BARNARD FORGED A NUMBER OF CLOSE FRIENDSHIPS WITH OTHER YOUNG PEOPLE HER AGE.

Beth was among three young women – all of whom had parents with houses on the island – who formed an inseparable bond.

During their early twenties, Beth, Margaret and Deborah spoke on the phone nearly every day and saw each other most weekends. Beth and Margaret met while working at the Penguin Parade while Deborah met the other two through her then husband who also worked with the penguins too.

The three shared their most intimate secrets and offered each other advice in times of trouble. They were so close in fact, that early on in their friendship, they resolved that, if one of them were to marry or remarry, the remaining two would be bridesmaids. They always vowed the bridesmaids would wear pink dresses.

'We told each other everything,' says Deborah.

In October 1985, a little less than a year before Beth's murder, the three women went for a two-week holiday to the Maldive Islands, off the coast of India. The reason for the trip was two-fold, says Deborah. Firstly, the young women were keen for a holiday and secondly, it would give Deborah and Beth an opportunity to think seriously about their respective complicated relationships: Deborah's marriage was rocky and Beth was having an affair with a married man, Fergus Cameron.

For the most part, they spent their time sunning themselves on the beaches, wandering the small villages and markets and going out together in the evenings. Photographs taken of Beth at the time testify to her healthy tan and relaxed, happy demeanour.

Every evening when the young women came home, they would sit around their hotel rooms talking about their aims and ambitions. According to Deborah, Beth confessed to her two friends that she was deeply in love with Fergus, but that she was loath to break up his family. Beth also told her friends that she also loved Fergus's two boys but, having witnessed marital tensions close to her own family, she thought that the interests of the children should come first.

Beth confessed to the others that she had never had a serious boyfriend before Fergus, who she described as her 'first true love'. Indeed, she told them that Fergus was the first man with whom she had had a sexual relationship.

By the end of their holiday, the three women had resolved to put their private lives into order. For Deborah this meant resolving her unhappy marriage while Beth, according to the other two, said she was again considering ending her relationship with Fergus.

Today Deborah and Margaret recall a curious incident on their holiday to the Maldives. At the time, they say, it was of little significance.

After they had gone to dinner one night, a palm reader approached them to offer his services. Somewhat flippantly they agreed on a price and showed their hands to the elderly Indian man who promised to predict their futures. Deborah and Margaret went first. They weren't too surprised when he promised them the usual: love, longevity and children. However, when Beth's turn came, the mystic took a quick look at her hand and refused to read her future. Despite their pleas that he read Beth's palm, the Indian man steadfastly refused, offering the repeated excuse that he was too tired. The girls laughed and thought nothing more of the incident.

Eleven months later – Beth was dead.

About five months after returning to Australia, Deborah left the country again for an extended stay in England. During her time in the United Kingdom, she received a number of letters and tapes from Beth and Margaret, who had remained on Phillip Island. Deborah still has a tape she received a short time after she arrived in England. Beth and Margaret were having dinner with Fergus and Margaret's fiancé, Robert. After setting the tape recorder on the dinner table, they all enjoyed a rowdy evening, talking among themselves and to Deborah about the most recent developments in their lives.

During the taped conversation Beth spoke about, among other things, the trouble her relationship with Fergus was causing her at work at the Penguin Parade.

'Work hasn't been too good for me,' says Beth on the tape. 'I've been pulled up into Peter's office the other night and given the run around and we found out what happened. How I got into trouble – he seemed to know everything I was doing – all about my personal life, and we found out that [Beth names a female co-worker] dobbed on me. She found out that I had a phone call from Fergus and she told Peter, and I got into trouble because I was seeing too much of Fergus.'

Listening to the tape in London, Deborah felt almost as if she was on Phillip Island, sitting around the table enjoying the company of her best friends.

A considerable part of their conversation was dedicated to a young man who lived on the Island who had developed an obsession with Beth. The women spoke about how this man would mow Beth's lawns when she was out, sit outside her house in his Land Cruiser at night and leave expensive bunches of flowers on her doorstep every couple of days. The man had been doing this for months because Deborah could remember that, even before she had left for England, Beth used to share the flowers with her and Margaret.

In the tape they recorded on the night of the dinner, Fergus jokes with Beth that he is surprised that she 'hasn't put up the sign'.

Beth laughs before explaining to Deborah: 'The sign that Fergus is talking about is a "No Right Turn After 5 PM" sign. They were going to put it up outside my house so that [the admirer] won't keep coming around.'

Laughing, Margaret responds to Beth saying, 'He spends days and nights here, Bethals.' Beth replies, 'I've got this problem how he keeps mowing my lawns, and I don't want him to, 'cause I feel as if I owe him something when he does it. And, he mowed them again on Monday and I get home and yelled at him and he got really pissed off and, so anyway he just took off and I thought "Oh beauty, I've got rid of him now". And he came back Monday night and got mad at me and, fair dinkum, I just feel like telling him where to go now, and then he came to work at Cameron's on Tuesday 'cause we were lamb marking and all day. I was in a real shit and I kept trying to find other jobs to do and he just comes and takes over my jobs and tells me what to do. Fergus thought I was being really good trying to do all these other things and I was just trying to get away and so I'm just sick of him [the admirer]. I wish they'd do something to stop him coming around. We gave him all these hints not to come around tonight, so if he comes, I think I'll just knock him out!'

Margaret speaks to Deborah on the tape: 'I don't know why she complains. I love having the flowers at my place. They're better off at my place than at the tip.'

While the antics of her admirer certainly annoyed Beth, she never indicated that she was afraid of him. Indeed, she had told him that while she liked him as a friend, there was no chance that their relationship would develop further. However, he persisted with the flowers, the lawn-mowing and his late night surveillance of Beth's house.

According to those who knew the young man, he was devastated by Beth's murder. Indeed, two days after she died, he placed a death notice in Melbourne's *Sun News-Pictorial*.

'Beth, you filled a very special place in my heart. I will always hold our special friendship close. You made my life complete.'

But it seems that wasn't his only response to Beth's death.

According to Deborah, the day after Beth's murder, the young man telephoned Margaret to discuss the killing. He allegedly asked Margaret if she had spoken to the police. When she said she hadn't, but expected to do so, he implored her not to talk to them. However, Margaret told him she would do 'anything possible' to help the detectives find the person who killed Beth. Perhaps he was worried that his actions would implicate him.

Although some of those closest to her would later tell police that Beth was careless when it came to personal security, there were indications in the tape recorded conversation sent to Deborah that the opposite was true.

In the tape Margaret asks Beth if she has let the dog inside – referring to Beth's nightly practice of keeping one of the farm dogs inside for security. Beth replies that she hasn't, but will later. Beth also told one of her dinner guests, Robert, who is proficient in martial arts: 'I'll get you to come and hold the door for me when some one comes and knocks on it, and hold my hand.'

Some time after Beth's death, Deborah reflected that Beth always kept at least one of the farm dogs in the house with her when she was home alone. 'She always kept the doors locked. She was very security conscious.'

If Beth inadvertently left her back door unlocked, she would have presented her killer with easy access to her home.

Chapter Four

Beth's Final Hours

BECAUSE BETH SPENT MUCH OF HER LAST DAY ALONE, IT IS DIFFICULT TO SAY EXACTLY WHAT HER MOVEMENTS WERE FOR MUCH OF THE DAY, AND WHO SHE SPOKE TO.

But one of her best friends, Margaret, spent a couple of hours with Beth – on Monday 22 September, 1986 – her last day on earth.

After the friends spoke on the phone in the morning, Beth arranged to visit Margaret at her house. It is evident from the contents of her handbag she carried, that Beth was still feeling the effects of the flu. She carried with her, among other things, some cough lollies, a packet of Moxacin capsules and Triphasil tablets.

Soon after Beth arrived at Margaret's house, the pair went to a nearby newsagency where they bought a number of women's magazines with a view to entering some of the competitions among the pages. The friends did this often, anticipating the overseas holidays and new cars they stood to win.

While they sat in Margaret's house, filling out the entry forms, Beth spoke about her relationship with Fergus and the evening she planned to spend with him.

Beth told Margaret that, once again, she was tired of the way her affair with Fergus was going and that she saw little future in the way it had developed during the past year or so.

While filling in the entry forms, Beth said that she planned to give Fergus an ultimatum over dinner that night. According to Margaret, Beth had every intention of telling Fergus that he would have to resolve his marital difficulties – one way or another. Beth saw no future in their relationship continuing with the way things were. Margaret appreciated how hard the situation had been for Beth. She could remember how upset Beth had been after Vivienne had caught Fergus warmly embracing Beth in the shearing shed. Margaret also knew that Beth would never intentionally break up a marriage. Beth had been deeply in love with Fergus and had always believed the Cameron marriage was 'finished' before her affair with Fergus had begun. It was a difficult time for Beth.

Beth told Margaret that her brother had intended to make the drive from Melbourne to Phillip Island where he would spend the night with her at the house in McFees Road. However, Margaret said, Beth's brother had broken his arm in an accident and had cancelled the trip.

Margaret said that Beth had assured her mother by phone that because her brother was not coming, she would bring the dogs inside as usual for extra protection.

Margaret said that Beth left her house early in the afternoon to return to McFees Road, so that she could prepare dinner for Fergus.

It was the last time Margaret would ever see her best friend.

The day Beth was murdered, Margaret telephoned Deborah at work in England and broke the news of the tragedy. Although she had only just arrived at work, Deborah left straight away to make arrangements to return to Australia for the funeral. When she got to her flat, she found a letter waiting for her. It was from Beth.

In the letter, Beth told Deborah that she was confused about her relationship with Fergus and wanted to get away from Phillip Island for a while. Beth wrote that she wanted to join Deborah in London for a holiday.

Through her tears, Deborah read the letter again and again. Despite her hasty travel plans, Deborah arrived in Melbourne too late for her best friend's funeral.

Chapter Five
Vivienne

VIVIENNE CAMERON BEGAN WORKING AT THE COWES COMMUNITY HOUSE IN SEPTEMBER 1984 – TWO YEARS BEFORE SHE DISAPPEARED.

Her job was to coordinate the various courses offered to Community House patrons – courses in craft or educational subjects. She was good at her job.

Such contact with members of her community helped Vivienne overcome her natural shyness. Vivienne enjoyed helping people, but she neither expected nor wanted the kudos that follows such good deeds. Her brother recalls a time before Vivienne was married, when she volunteered to teach English to migrants at night classes. Vivienne never told anyone about her work. She just got on with her job. In essence, Vivienne was a quiet achiever.

Vivienne Cameron grew up in the country and quickly adapted to married life with her husband Fergus, and worked on the family farm. She didn't shy from the laborious tasks but embraced the hard work, even after the birth of her two children. Friends remember her driving the family Land Cruiser around the property and unloading hay bales while her two youngsters rode with her, and recall the youngest child nearby in a pusher while she gave the sheep immunisation needles.

Many friends recall Vivienne's dry sense of humour. One colleague was handing out 'pro-choice' abortion pamphlets at a political meeting, and remembered meeting Vivienne. Vivienne's reaction was immediate – she roared laughing. She quickly explained that she found it extremely funny to see the woman handing out such pamphlets to the many staunchly conservative locals. Vivienne loved to see the establishment – to which she, by way of her marriage, belonged – challenged.

Vivienne told the same friend that she loved her job because it gave her the opportunity to meet people outside her family's social circle. Other friends testify to her great sympathy for those less fortunate than herself.

One young mother on the island spent a lot of time with Vivienne as their children were the same age. The friend recalls visiting Vivienne often at her farm and describes her as 'very quietly spoken yet quietly confident'. This friend also says that Vivienne was very much a part of the farm business and management.

All of Vivienne's friends bear witness to her great love for her children and many have memories of the enjoyable birthday parties she used to have for them. Vivienne's children were relatively unrestricted. They lived on a large farm and they had a free run, but Vivienne was never far away.

The murder of Beth Barnard shocked all Vivienne's friends. Her possible involvement perplexed them. Outside very restricted circles in Australian society – the insanely violent and professionally criminal circles, for example, are obvious exceptions – one seldom expects the people one knows to murder. But even so, Vivienne Cameron seemed, as one Islander put it, 'the last person you'd expect to kill someone'.

One friend was driving to school to give her son his lunch when she heard the news on the radio. The friends had known of Beth's murder, but had no idea that Vivienne was in any way connected. 'I burst into tears and had to drive straight home again,' said the friend.

Vivienne's colleagues at the Community House just couldn't believe it either. Another friend recalled sadly that Vivienne was supposed to have been on 'milk and fruit' duty at her son's kindergarten on the day she vanished.

Just a few weeks after Vivienne disappeared, her husband Fergus held a Memorial Service at their farmhouse. Those who attended remember many cars lined up on the surrounding paddocks – it was a big turn-out.

Dr Paul Flood, among others, spoke to the large gathering about the friend they had lost. Vivienne's children planted roses to remember their mother. One woman who attended the service felt awkward. She felt that the service was premature – Vivienne may yet come back. But she did recognise the benefit of such a service to the two children who had lost their mother.

Chapter Six

The Nets Are Cast

WHENEVER A MURDER IS REPORTED, A CRIME SCENE EXAMINER FROM THE
VICTORIA POLICE STATE FORENSIC SCIENCE LABORATORY MUST ATTEND.

The crime scene examiner, while never among the first to arrive
at the murder scene, carries out one of the most important jobs in
the investigation.

On Tuesday 23 September, 1986, local police and homicide
squad detectives had already been at Beth's house in Rhyll for
five hours, when Sergeant Hughie Peters and Senior Constable
Brian Gamble arrived from Melbourne to take charge of the
forensic team.

Hughie Peters and Brian Gamble didn't work alone. The team
that attended the murder scene at McFees Road, Rhyll consisted
of Sergeant Michael Rilen and Senior Constable Stephen Jones –
both from the fingerprint bureau, Senior Constable Peter Gates

from the photographic section and Hank Otterspoor and Trevor
Beattie from the audio visual section of the Forensic Science
Laboratory. It was the duty of Otterspoor and Beattie to videotape
the crime scene for police records, while Peter Gates took the crime
scene photographs.

Brian Gamble and Hughie Peters were there to oversee the
collection of evidence at Barnard farmhouse and to meticulously
take note of anything that could be relevant to the investigation.
While the homicide squad detectives were concentrating on
motives and looking for possible murder suspects, Gamble and
Peters looked for pieces of physical evidence, for example: any
item stained with blood, possible murder weapons, fingerprints
or any letters or diaries belonging to Beth. These items were all
carefully sealed in either plastic or paper bags and sent to the
Victoria Police State Forensic Science Laboratory in Macleod, an
outer northern suburb of Melbourne, for analysis.

Gamble and Peters were given a brief outline of the facts
surrounding the murder as far as the detectives themselves knew.
They were told that the major suspect was Vivienne Cameron,
that Vivienne had disappeared and the police were searching for
her.

Brian Gamble later explained that the crime scene examiner
'starts at the body and works his way out' when beginning an
examination. The areas immediately around Beth's body were the
initial focus as was the whole of her bedroom. The rest of the house
would come later.

Unlike some other police, Brian Gamble wasn't shocked when
he first saw the body of Beth Barnard. To him, it was a part of his
job and he studied the body with detached, professional interest.
The blood smears all over her body, he thought, were too many in
number and covered too large an area to have been caused

incidentally in the frenzied attack. He thought that perhaps the murderer had rubbed his or her blood-soaked hands all over the surface of Beth's arms and legs to cause the extensive smearing. The thought wasn't a pleasant one.

Gamble's experience of murder also led him to form the opinion that the disfigurement to Beth's face – the stab wounds in her upper lip and chin, and the knocking out of her front tooth – was probably deliberate. He thought, from experience, that whoever killed Beth had probably hated her and not only wanted her dead but also to destroy her physical beauty and attraction.

He described Beth's body in his notes: 'The deceased was a female lying on her back. She was wearing a blood-soaked pink T-shirt and a pair of white and blue striped pants. The T-shirt was pulled up at the front exposing her stomach, chest and right breast. Heavy blood smears were apparent on the deceased's arms, face, neck, chest and abdomen and thighs. On the carpet between the deceased's left shoulder and the left side of her head, was a pool of congealed blood.

'I observed the following wounds to the deceased. Her throat had been cut. She had a cut in her top lip and cuts on the inside of her fingers on both hands. What appeared to be a large letter "A" had been carved into her chest.'

Gamble was required to lodge a report with both the Victoria Police State Forensic Science Laboratory and the homicide squad, and he meticulously collected exhibits, labelled all of the bags and carefully noted the exact places where the evidence was collected. This was important because, when the bags reached the laboratory scientists, they needed to have exact records of where each of the bagged items came from, and the police needed their own records. In this case, Gamble knew this methodical process was especially important because of the number of articles gathered as evidence

– there would eventually be about 70 items, including: the continental quilt cover which was draped over Beth's body, a wooden-handled knife found near the body, every blood-splattered piece of clothing that had lain on the floor during the struggle, cigarette butts and bathroom towels and even a tap knob from the bathroom.

While overseeing the collection of evidence inside the house, Gamble made rough sketches of the full floor-plan. The sketches included a separate drawing of Beth's room and the position of her body. In his notes, in addition to his sketches, he also wrote descriptions: 'Victim's head positioned virtually in doorway. Body draped with a floral covered doona. Security door fitted – no sign of forced entry. Bedroom untidy, but no obvious signs of a struggle. Heavy bloodstaining apparent on the folded part of the top blanket and the bottom sheet [of Beth's bed]'.

Gamble's experience with crime scenes told him that the small ornaments on Beth's cluttered chest of drawers would have been knocked over without much difficulty in even the slightest of struggles. The fact they were all still standing led him to conclude that, while Beth had obviously defended herself, there had been no great struggle. Even the small bedside lamp, still shedding a dim light across the room, appeared undisturbed.

It was also Gamble's job to try to establish where Beth's killer entered the house. He checked every window and door, finding them all [except the back door] closed and locked. He noted that dust around the windows hadn't been disturbed, indicating to him that nobody had forced their way in.

He walked out the back door to take a close look around the outside of the Barnard's farmhouse. As he purposefully made his way around the property, Gamble made more sketches of the backyard and directed Peter Gates, the police photographer, to take pictures of all tyre-mark impressions in the long driveway leading to the house. Unfortunately, when Sergeant Cliff Ashe had followed Ian Cairns and Donald Cameron to the house earlier that morning, both vehicles had driven up the dirt driveway. All of the tyre impressions noted and photographed would later be compared with those of vehicles belonging to Vivienne and Fergus Cameron.

Having been told about the two small drops of blood on the path leading from the back door, Gamble carefully took scrapings of both the blood and some unstained concrete, to use as a control in the forensic testing. These scrapings were put into bags, labelled and numbered.

Also outside, under a back carport, Gamble inspected two vehicles. One was Beth's car – a Mazda 323 – and the other was a Toyota ute also belonging to the Barnards. Ashtrays in both vehicles contained cigarette butts. Gamble determined that they were mostly Peter Stuyvesant brand butts and he also found an empty packet of Peter Stuyvesant cigarettes on the dashboard of the Mazda. He made a careful note of these brands.

Meanwhile the officers from the fingerprint bureau, Stephen Jones and Michael Rilen, using both black and white dust, carefully developed fingerprints – some of them found on Beth's chest of drawers. Rilen and Jones labelled these prints and carefully photographed them with their own Polaroid camera. The prints were later compared with the fingerprints Detective Rory O'Connor had taken from Beth after the autopsy. Rilen found that the fingerprints on the chest of drawers belonged to Beth.

Rilen and Jones also tested Beth's body for fingerprints. The skin of a living or dead body can produce identifiable latent fingerprints if dusted soon enough after contact. One of the few cases where fingerprint officers have lifted identifiable fingerprints from the skin of a victim was in the United States. A rape victim, who had just attended a gym workout prior to her attack, was successfully fingerprinted. The officers found that because her skin was sweaty from her workout, she retained her attacker's prints. The rapist was subsequently identified. Such cases of officers lifting useable prints from victims is rare, however, fingerprint experts always try.

The two officers from the fingerprint branch could easily see that the killer had wiped their hands on Beth's arms, legs and torso, and as was usual practice in such cases, they sprinkled a black magnetic metal powder on sections of her body. This so-called Magna powder is finer in quality to the normal fingerprint dust used on other surfaces. It adheres to the skin and, if prints are on the skin surface, they appear highlighted by the dark powder. Rilen and Jones dusted Magna powder over Beth's body – on the surfaces not covered by hair which prevents prints making any impression on the skin itself. They found no distinguishable fingerprints.

It was not unusual for the officers from the fingerprint branch not to find the killer's prints at a crime scene. According to experts, not everybody leaves fingerprints all the time. Some manual labourers such as bricklayers, can wear their prints down so as to be almost nonexistent. Chemicals in household cleansers can also reduce the amount of moisture in the fingertips, as can a person's emotional state, thus reducing the clarity of the print. The more moisture, the better the print.

No fingerprints were found on what was accepted to have been the murder weapon – the large knife found beside Beth in her bedroom – or in the bloodied hand marks around the bathroom basin. The knife hadn't been wiped as it was still heavily bloodstained – the killer hadn't left prints.

The forensic team worked late into the night in their search for clues. Brian Gamble later admitted that a certain eerie feeling prevailed among the team, alone in the isolated farmhouse as darkness descended, with a killer on the loose.

When their work was finished for the night, the tired forensic team stayed in a motel in San Remo.

Homicide Squad detectives O'Connor and Hunter had left the forensic team in the early afternoon to begin interviewing Beth's neighbours in McFees Road. Their first stop was the Barnard's closest neighbour, a waitress called Dianne who lived with her friend, Joyce. Although she had been curious about the police cars outside Beth's house and the many men in suits wandering about the property, Dianne was shocked to hear there had been a murder next door. Consequently, she had little information for the detectives. However, she did remember seeing a car drive up McFees Road towards the Barnard house when she had walked outside the previous evening. Because there were only seven farmhouses in McFees Road, traffic was rare and cars that didn't belong to residents were usually noticed.

Dianne remembered this car clearly because she had thought it was going to turn into her own driveway. She told O'Connor and Hunter that she had stood outside her house and continued to watch the parked car, with casual interest, because the headlights stayed on for several minutes, before being extinguished. She had wondered why. Because she had been due to go out in 30 minutes, Dianne noted the time was 7.50pm. She told the detectives that, when she left the house again half an hour later, she didn't notice if the car was still in Beth's driveway. She explained that she had only seen the car headlights through a row of tall trees which lined the side of Beth's driveway nearest Dianne's house.

Rory O'Connor and Garry Hunter decided to try a house on the other side of the Barnard property, towards the dead-end of McFees Road. The house belonged to an elderly woman, Margaret McFee, and her husband, after whose family the road had been named. Mrs McFee was extremely upset to hear that the young woman who lived almost across the road had been killed. Beth had often walked across – and just up the road – to share a pot of tea and have a chat with Mrs McFee.

The detectives waited patiently for the elderly woman to compose herself and listened intently when she explained about the car she had heard the night before. 'I had just woken up as I usually do in the middle of the night, to go to the toilet and I heard a car drive past. It was a loud one and the lights shone right into my bedroom window. It sounded a bit like my son's Toyota Tray [truck],' Mrs McFee said. 'I was a bit worried you see, because my sister-in-law lives at the end of the road by herself, and I'm very conscious of vehicles going to the end of the road. I waited for it to come back and within a few minutes it did, so I didn't think anything of it, and I went back to sleep.'

Mrs McFee shuddered involuntarily as she spoke to the detectives, realising that the car could have carried Beth's murderer.

'Thanks for your help Mrs McFee,' said O'Connor, 'we'll send around another detective in the next couple of days to take a written statement.' The detectives noted the importance of Margaret McFee's information and left her alone with her grief.

Margaret McFee's sister-in-law, Eileen 'Cherry' McFee, was also visited by the detectives. She told them she had taken her dog for a walk shortly after 8 o'clock that morning. 'As I walked through the front gate, I noticed tyre skid marks on the front lawn area. I noticed that it was fresh because I am conscious of keeping everything nice because I am having a wedding at the house on the weekend coming.'

Cherry McFee told the detectives that her sister-in-law, Margaret, had come to visit her soon after her walk and told her about the car she heard in the very early hours of the morning. 'I realised that the skid marks must have been made by that vehicle. The skid marks were definitely not there the night before because I mowed... I like to keep everything nice.'

The detectives thanked her for her time.

O'Connor and Hunter drove to the Cameron house in Watts Road, Ventnor to collect photographs of Vivienne Cameron to circulate with the 'missing person' bulletin. O'Connor and Hunter then drove to their temporary headquarters, the Cowes Police Station, to plan their course of action. When they arrived, Detective Jack McFayden was in another room where he had just started formally interviewing Donald Cameron.

'Have a seat, Don,' said McFayden, offering Cameron a chair in the interview room. McFayden had only heard the short version of the events that had taken place at McFees Road in the early hours of the morning. He was expecting Donald Cameron to enlighten him further.

'Tell me in your own words, Donald, what you know about this business,' began McFayden, who had settled into another chair, his pen poised, as Donald began: 'At approximately 7.45 this morning, I received a phone call from Mrs Robyn Dixon, who is a close family friend. She was concerned because she hadn't heard from Fergus and Viv, and she couldn't get them on the phone. She said she had the children with her. As she had to go to work, she said she'd put the school-aged child on the bus with her two boys, and I told her not to worry, I would come to pick up the other child.'

He collected the boy. Then Cameron explained that he'd driven home past Fergus's house and noticed that Vivienne's Holden Sedan was still in the driveway. 'I got home and my wife Pam rang my sister Marnie, and Fergus answered the phone,' Donald Cameron said.

'He seemed really distressed and didn't want to talk to us, so he handed the phone to Marnie's husband Ian. Ian diplomatically told Pam that something had happened and he would talk to us later. Pam insisted that we know what had happened because we had their child with us.

'Fergus then got back on the phone and told Pam that there had been a row the night before and he had been injured and had to be treated at the hospital. We gathered that the row had been of a domestic nature and it had involved Beth Barnard. But other than that, Fergus was pretty uncommunicative.'

Donald Cameron told McFayden that Ian Cairns had phoned back a short time later to say that Fergus's Land Cruiser was missing from its usual spot in Fergus's machinery shed. Ian Cairns told him that Fergus wanted them to tell Beth about the fight the night before.

'Ian asked me to go with him to Beth's place,' Donald Cameron told McFayden. 'I picked Ian up a couple of minutes later and I saw Fergus briefly at the back door.' McFayden paid particular attention when Don described his brother as looking 'very distressed'. On the way to Beth's, Donald told McFayden that he and Ian had first called into Fergus and Vivienne's house. They walked inside and called out for Vivienne but, said Donald, the house had been empty. They then headed for McFees Road, Rhyll.

'We drove up the driveway and saw Beth's farm ute and her own car parked in their usual spots. I walked to the back door and knocked but there was no answer. The porch light was on and I saw that the door was open about six inches. I called out but there was no answer,' Donald Cameron told McFayden.

'I took a step inside and saw the [bedroom] door to my left. Just beyond the door, I saw Beth lying there on the floor covered with a quilt. Her face was almost covered but I recognised her and she appeared to be dead. I yelled out to Ian: "Come here quick, the worst has happened". We immediately left to report what we'd found at the Cowes police station. That's really all I can tell you.'

Donald Cameron rose to go but McFayden wanted to know more. 'I'll keep in touch Don,' he said to Cameron's surprise, as if he were wondering what more the police could possibly want from him. He signed the statement that McFayden had written, after reading it through carefully. McFayden noted the time at the bottom of the statement. It was 12.50pm.

As soon as Don Cameron had left, McFayden went into O'Connor's temporary office.

'What do you think?' he asked O'Connor, who had been talking with Detective Hunter.

'Pretty weird,' he replied.

'Yeah,' said McFayden. 'I've never seen a bunch of people so cool, calm and collected. You'd think these blokes discovered bodies every day of their lives.'

Chapter Seven

A Phone Call in the Night

JACK McFAYDEN KNEW ALREADY, FROM HIS INTERVIEW WITH DONALD CAMERON, THAT ROBYN DIXON HAD COLLECTED VIVIENNE AND FERGUS'S CHILDREN AT SOME STAGE ON THE NIGHT BETH WAS MURDERED.

But he wanted to know more about the phone call that Vivienne made to Robyn, and whether she had noticed anything suspicious when she went to get the two kids.

McFayden told detectives O'Connor and Hunter that he was going over to the San Remo Primary School, where Mrs Dixon worked as a relieving teacher, to get a statement from her.

'Apparently she received a phone call from Vivienne Cameron

around three this morning. She's the one who picked up the Cameron kids,' McFayden told the two detectives. O'Connor thought about this for a moment: Margaret McFee – the elderly neighbour of Beth's – had told him and Hunter earlier that day, that she had heard a car drive past her house at 3.20am. It figured, he thought, that if Vivienne was driving that car, she would have had plenty of time to call Robyn Dixon at 3am and be at Beth's 20 minutes later. If this was the case, thought O'Connor, the evidence was stacking up against Vivienne Cameron, who still hadn't been found.

Afternoon classes had just begun at the small San Remo Primary School when Detective McFayden walked into the school office and asked to see Mrs Robyn Dixon. After identifying himself as a policeman and explaining the urgency and nature of his visit, Mrs Dixon was quickly summoned from her class.

After introducing himself to Mrs Dixon, McFayden explained: 'I'm here to ask you a few questions in relation to the murder of a young woman on Phillip Island last night. Elizabeth Barnard was found dead at her parents' house in Rhyll this morning. I hope you can help me.'

While information surrounding Beth's murder was spreading quickly on the Island, Mrs Dixon, who had been at school since about 8.30 that morning, was shocked to hear the news. Even though Robyn hadn't been a close friend of Beth's, she had seen her working around the Cameron's farm when she had gone to visit Vivienne.

After composing herself, Mrs Dixon asked: 'How can I help you?'

McFayden explained that Fergus's brother, Donald, had said that Mrs Dixon had received a phone call from Vivienne early that morning. Vivienne had apparently wanted Robyn to collect her two children because she was at the hospital with Fergus.

'That's right,' said Mrs Dixon. 'My husband, John, answered the phone. Vivienne said she was calling from the hospital, which I assumed was Cowes. She said that the children were at her home and asked me to get them and take them home for the night. We agreed to this and John asked if everything was all right. But I can't recall what she said.'

John Dixon hadn't wanted to go to Fergus and Vivienne's by himself, for fear of frightening the two children, and he hadn't wanted Robyn to go on her own, so they had both decided to go, Mrs Dixon told McFayden. They got there about 10 minutes later, woke the children and took them home.

'Did you notice anything unusual at the Camerons' house?' McFayden asked. '...I noticed that their cream Holden Kingswood sedan was in the garage and I thought that this was unusual. I thought they might have been picked up by an ambulance or a relation,' she replied.

He asked her if she'd noticed anything inside the house.

'The back porch light, the bathroom light, and a little room light were on in the house and everything appeared normal and I saw Vivienne's handbag was on the table inside the back door. I assumed it was Vivienne's handbag, although I'm not sure, I know it was of black suede. This made me think she left in a hurry,' Mrs Dixon said.

Mrs Dixon didn't mention seeing any of the blood that was later found in the hallway, bedroom and bathroom of the Cameron house.

In her statement to McFayden, Robyn Dixon said that at 7.30 that morning she had tried to ring Vivienne, but there was no answer. She then tried to ring Donald Cameron, but the line was engaged. When she eventually got through to Donald 15 minutes later, she explained that she was in a hurry to get to work but that she still had the children with her.

'Donald said he didn't know what I was talking about when I asked who was sick, and he put Pam on the phone to speak to me. I told Pam about the phone call from Viv at 3am, telling me that they were at the hospital. I told Pam that I still had the children and I had to get to work. Pam arranged for Donald to pick up the little one, who is five years old and I was to take the older child with my children to the bus,' she said.

McFayden thought this was unusual because Donald Cameron had told him that before he answered Mrs Dixon's phone call at 7.45am, he had no knowledge that anything was amiss. Who then, McFayden wondered, had Donald Cameron or his wife, Pam, been speaking to for the 15 minutes or more that morning when Robyn Dixon was trying to call them?

Donald Cameron's wife, Pamela, first met Beth Barnard in 1984, when Beth began working as a part-time farmhand on Fergus and Vivienne's property. The three adult Cameron siblings – Fergus, Donald and Marnie – and their respective spouses formed a close-knit clan, so it's not surprising that Pamela considered Beth to be an employee of the whole family, rather than just her brother-in-law.

In the two years since they had first met, Pamela and Beth had become close friends. Pamela would later say that Beth was considered to be part of the family and that she affectionately referred to Donald Cameron as 'Uncle Donald' or 'Grandpa'. Pamela's children treated Beth as a sister.

Pamela, a physiotherapist who worked at the San Remo District Community Health Centre, developed a close friendship with the young farmhand when she began treating her for a back injury.

Despite her strong friendship with Beth, she remained oblivious to the intimate relationship between Beth and her brother-in-law, Fergus. In the 11 years since Fergus and Vivienne had been married, Pam had, from time to time, been aware of problems in their relationship. Occasionally their marital problems had culminated in arguments in front of other members of the family. However, during these arguments, Pamela had never heard Beth Barnard's name mentioned.

In a short period before Beth's murder, Pamela had even noticed that Vivienne and Fergus's marriage appeared to have strengthened.

Pamela had just taken a lunch break at the health centre when a work colleague told her that a young woman had been found dead at a house in McFees Road, Rhyll. Because of the phone conversation she and Donald had with Fergus earlier that day, and knowing where her close friend Beth lived, she immediately rang her husband. Donald confirmed the worst.

Donald also told his wife that Vivienne had disappeared along with Fergus's Land Cruiser and that the police were looking for her. Pamela immediately arranged to finish work earlier than usual. However, she was still unable to get away until almost 4pm.

Knowing that she'd spoken to Fergus earlier that morning, Jack McFayden was intending to interview Pamela Cameron when, about an hour after Pamela left work, he answered the phone at Cowes Police Station. It was Pamela's brother-in-law, Ian Cairns, who had called to say that Pamela had spotted Fergus's Land Cruiser.

Ten minutes later McFayden and the two homicide squad detectives arrived at Forrest Avenue in Newhaven, to find the Land Cruiser parked on a wide nature strip adjoining a playground.

Some detectives assigned to the case would later say that a local baker, Wayne Hunt, who had been doing his early morning deliveries, had first seen the Land Cruiser at five that morning. The detectives treated this piece of information as vital because, if the car was there that early it was, to them and subsequently the coroner, a strong indication that Vivienne Cameron had committed suicide by jumping from the bridge.

Indeed, to this day the theory that Vivienne jumped from the bridge is based largely on the premise that Hunt saw the Land Cruiser early on the morning of Vivienne's disappearance. However, this premise – and subsequently the suicide theory if it is based on this premise alone – is fatally flawed.

An examination of Hunt's statement, taken by detective Garry Hunter on 27 September, 1986, reveals that Hunt may not have seen the Land Cruiser at all that morning. Indeed, it is clear from his statement that Hunt took little notice of whatever type of vehicle it was that had been parked near the bridge that morning.

'I cannot say what type of car it was or colour, all I can say is that there was a car parked there,' Hunt said in his statement.

'I just glanced and kept on going, but thought it was strange for it to be parked there at that time because normally there is nothing there. I thought it must have been someone using the toilet and didn't think any more about it.'

However, that afternoon it was clearly the Cameron's Land Cruiser parked in Forrest Avenue. Ironically the Land Cruiser could be clearly seen from the Phillip Island end of the bridge and if it had been there since early morning the detectives, driving back and forth from Wonthaggi and Melbourne, had passed it, unnoticed, many times during the day.

The car was locked. But McFayden already knew from his phone conversation with Ian Cairns that it was Pamela who had locked it. McFayden and the other detectives still weren't sure why she'd done that.

However, in her later statement, Mrs Cameron said after she left work about 4pm she noticed the Land Cruiser near the playground. She made a U-turn and, realising it was indeed the car belonging to her family, parked her car and got out for a closer inspection. She noticed that the windows were open and the keys were still in the ignition. She also saw a gold Oroton purse and a black handbag on the seat.

One of the first things she also noticed were several packets of cigarettes: on the dashboard was a full packet and on the seat, an opened packet and a lighter. Both packets were Claridge, she knew – the brand smoked by her sister-in-law, Vivienne. She said another set of keys, which opened the gates to the family's motor racing track, were also on the dash.

Pamela Cameron assumed the detectives had already found the Land Cruiser and her sister-in-law Vivienne, because during her lunch hour, while driving to a pottery shop in Newhaven she had seen a police car near the Phillip Island end of the bridge. Rationalising that the police took Vivienne and left the car open, Pamela Cameron said she took the keys out of the ignition and the gold purse, before going back to work to ring her husband. Donald Cameron told her to tell the police at San Remo that she'd found the Land Cruiser.

After driving to the unattended police station, she returned to the Land Cruiser and removed the race track keys. As she was about to lock the driver's side door, Pamela noticed a carving knife with a black handle on the passenger side floor, on top of a pair of Drizabone trousers.

'The knife was clean and I recognised it as one of Fergus and Vivienne's kitchen carving knives. We also have a set the same,' she said later in her statement. 'I opened the glove box to see if there was anything else valuable and I shut it again and then I locked the passenger side door.'

After locking the Land Cruiser, Pamela Cameron drove to the home of her brother-in-law, Ian Cairns. The three branches of the Cameron family all lived in Watts Road, Ventnor. She explained her find to Ian, who called the Cowes Police Station and spoke to McFayden.

While Ian Cairns spoke to the detective, Pamela opened the gold purse and found Vivienne's licence and a couple of plastic cards. Besides some loose change, there was no other money in the purse.

While McFayden, O'Connor and Hunter searched the Land Cruiser, they began to ponder, more seriously, the fate of Vivienne Cameron.

The car was parked only metres from a bus stop, but it was also less than several hundred metres from the start of the bridge. McFayden immediately searched the bridge for any signs that Vivienne may have jumped. Passing motorists noticed the lone detective as he slowly walked the narrow paths along both sides of the bridge. His well-trained eyes examined the white railing and searching for any blood or hair, a piece of clothing, shoes – anything that might indicate Vivienne had jumped the 10 metres to the icy water below. He found nothing.

While he searched the bridge, McFayden also considered the possibility that Vivienne had caught a bus at the last stop on Phillip Island. She could be anywhere by now, he thought. But most of all, Detective Jack McFayden wondered why detectives hadn't spotted Fergus and Vivienne Cameron's Land Cruiser earlier.

Besides Pamela Cameron, another person had seen the Land Cruiser which, unbeknown to the police, was parked near the bridge. John Dixon, a farmer and the husband of Robyn Dixon – who had collected the Cameron children from their parents' home early on 23 September – later told detectives he saw what looked like the Camerons' Land Cruiser parked in Forrest Avenue about 3pm on the same day.

Chapter Eight

The Crime Scene Examiner

CRIME SCENE EXAMINER, BRIAN GAMBLE'S WORK BEGAN AGAIN EARLY ON WEDNESDAY MORNING, 24 SEPTEMBER. HE WAS ASKED TO ATTEND THE SAN REMO POLICE STATION TO INSPECT THE LAND CRUISER FOUND NEAR THE PHILLIP ISLAND-SAN REMO BRIDGE THE PREVIOUS AFTERNOON.

At 8am Gamble arrived at the police station with fellow crime scene examiner, Sergeant Hughie Peters, Senior Constable Peter Gates from the photograph section of the Victoria Police State Forensic Science Laboratory with Sergeant Michael Rilen and Senior Constable Stephen Jones from the fingerprint branch.

Senior Constable Gates took three photographs of the Land Cruiser – one showing the vehicle with its number plate in view and another showing the inside of the vehicle and its contents strewn across its seats and floor. The third photograph was a close up of one of the Land Cruiser's tyres, which would later be compared with plaster casts taken from Beth Barnard's driveway.

When the photographer had finished, Gamble collected, labelled and bagged: a towel found on the floor of the Land Cruiser, a black handbag from the passenger seat, and a large, dirty, black-handled kitchen carving knife that lay beside the towel on the floor.

Gamble also collected two packets of Claridge brand cigarettes and a box of matches.

When the crime scene officers and the photographers were finished, Rilen and Jones dusted the Land Cruiser for fingerprints. No distinguishable prints were found, but this didn't surprise Sergeant Rilen, as the Land Cruiser was dusty and it had been locked up for two days in the sun. Rilen later explained that fingerprints are made up of water, salt and fats. If fingerprints are exposed to a warm or hot environment, they can literally dry up. Rilen remembers the weather to have been quite warm.

At 9.30am Gamble returned to continue his examination of the Barnard property in McFees Road, Rhyll. There, he collected two more pieces of evidence – a note pad and some cigarette butts that he found near the telephone, on the kitchen bench. He would later send the note pad for examination. Although there was no writing on the pages, the indentations of words from earlier pages could be studied for possible clues.

Gamble later gave the pad to Senior Constable Caroline Collins of the Document Examination Branch of the Victoria Police State Forensic Science Laboratory. Her tests would later show Beth had been working on what looked like a work budget, had written a shopping list, and that she had also written two reminder notes to herself: 'Post Deborah's letter', and 'Ring Margaret about dinner on Saturday night'.

The cigarette butts would also be important because Beth was a non-smoker and, therefore, they must have belonged to somebody else. Gamble concluded of the cigarette butts that those found on the kitchen bench, near the telephone, were Claridge – the brand smoked by Vivienne Cameron. However, Gamble identified the cigarette butt found in an ashtray in the bathroom – where the killer had apparently washed after cutting Beth's throat – as a Peter Stuyvesant brand.

Rilen and Jones tested the telephone for prints and found none that were for any use in identification.

The next day Gates took photographs of all of the tyre impressions in the long driveway of the Barnard farmhouse. Gamble later concluded from plaster casts he made of the tyre impressions that the partial tyre impressions could have been made with a vehicle fitted with Dunlop 'SP Roadgripper' tyres.

At 11.50am, Gamble and Gates arrived at the home of Fergus and Vivienne Cameron in Ventnor. As he had just done at Beth's house, Gamble sketched the surrounding property and the plan of the house. As he walked slowly from room to room, he looked carefully around, collecting evidence and taking elaborate notes.

Meanwhile, Gates took photographs, 15 in all, capturing such things as: the outside of the house, the kitchen area, a close up of a packet of Claridge brand cigarettes on the kitchen bench, a knife in the kitchen sink, bloodstains in the hallway and spare bedroom, the bathroom and the pink bloodstained tissue that Fergus said he had used to stem the flow of blood from his cut ear, bloodstains on the floor in the bathroom, bloodstained clothing in the laundry and also the Cameron's Holden Kingswood with its bloodstained front passenger seat.

Inside the Cameron house Gamble immediately noticed the blood splatters when he walked through the doorway of the front, spare bedroom. His notes record: 'I then entered the front spare bedroom. The doorway to this bedroom led from an area near the eastern end of the central hallway. The furniture consisted of a double bed with the head of the bed positioned up against the room's southern wall. Also against the southern wall was a wardrobe. In the north western corner of the room was a chest of drawers, a book case and a desk and a chair. Scattered over the bed were a number of papers. I observed a number of bloodstains in the room. On the floor between the western side of the bed and the western wall, were a number of blood droplets. On the bed spread and papers on the bed were a number of blood droplets. On the front of the chest of drawers was a blood smear'. Gates photographed the room and its bloodstained items.

Gamble left the front bedroom and continued his observations in the hallway: 'On the outside part of the door was a blood smear. I collected the following blood samples from this room...' He listed items such as two sheets of paper [from the bed], and scrapings of blood from the chest of drawers, the doorway and the wall in the hallway. After finishing with the front room, Gamble collected further items from around the house.

He took the pink tissues from the Camerons' bathroom stained with Fergus's blood, and some clothes found in the Camerons' laundry basket. He also took a scraping of blood from some droplets near the shower and toilet. In the kitchen, Gamble collected a sponge and a knife from near the sink.

At 1.55pm, Gates photographed Fergus Cameron's wounds. He took three photographs showing a front shot of Fergus

Cameron, a side view of his injured ear, and finally a view of the lacerations on his back which had been stitched by Dr Allan Powles two nights ago.

Later, Gamble would take the bloodstained knife, found next to Beth's body, into the fingerprint bureau where it was examined by Sergeant Michael Rilen, a policeman with seven years' experience in the examination and identification of fingerprints. According to Rilen's report, he was 'unable to obtain any fingerprints on this knife'. Rilen sent the knife back to Gamble to be analysed for blood types along with the other evidence.

Mid-afternoon, Gamble was required to attend the autopsy at the Korumburra District Hospital, where it was his job to collect other evidence such as Beth's nightshirt and her underwear – as well as samples removed from her body during her post-mortem examination. It was Gates's job to capture on film all of the injuries sustained by Beth on the night of her murder.

Chapter Nine

Stainless Steel and Plastic Aprons

THE JOB OF PERFORMING THE POST-MORTEM EXAMINATION OF ELIZABETH KATHERINE BARNARD WAS GIVEN TO DR G R ANDERSON, A MEDICAL PRACTITIONER FROM WARRAGUL, BY ORDER OF THE CORONER.

The post-mortem examination was carried out in the mortuary of the Korumburra District Hospital, in the early afternoon of Wednesday 24 September 1986.

Beth's body had been brought to the mortuary cool room only after it had been photographed, videoed and examined in situ. The scientific and forensic examiners had spent many hours going through the house to gather evidence and photographs and a video recording would keep, forever, a record of the crime scene.

At 3pm, detectives Rory O'Connor, Alan McFayden, Brian Gamble, and photographer Peter Gates attended the post-mortem to view Dr Andersen's examination. Throughout the examination, Gates would take nine graphic photographs.

The police officers were directed to the mortuary room by the hospital receptionist. The mortuary room was typical of the facilities available in a country hospital. Its facilities consisted of a metal trolley, a set of shining instruments for the pro-section, a bench and a sink. The room was lit by fluorescent bulbs. The olfactory senses of the detectives were immediately assaulted with the strong odour of disinfectant. When they arrived, a mortuary assistant, who had been busy laying out the instruments, walked over and opened a huge fridge and removed Beth Barnard's naked blood-smeared body which was reposing on a metal slab.

The assistant wheeled the metal trolley over to the fridge and roughly transferred the body onto the trolley and pushed it over to the small table where the instruments were.

'Shit,' said McFayden looking at the dead woman's body. McFayden was overwhelmed with the sadness permeating the scene. This young woman with so much promise was now lying before them – naked and hideously abused. There was no room for modesty or secrets now. The doctor would soon arrive to probe, measure, and cut.

That Beth Barnard had been stabbed to death was obvious to anyone, and nothing more could be done for her. But establishing how and when she died, or any oddities, might help with the last act society required: catching who killed her.

'Mmm, nasty,' muttered Doctor Anderson, heralding his arrival. He stood for a moment surveying the body in front of him. 'I don't like these Coroner's cases. What do you need?'

O'Connor took the lead: 'Doctor, we need the approximate time of death, an accurate description of every wound, and it would help if you could tell us which of the wounds was the fatal one. It would also help if we knew whether the "A" was carved before or after death. We need to know what kind of offender we're after.'

'That's a pretty tall order. I haven't done too many of these. I'll see what I can do,' said the doctor dressing himself in a green surgical gown. He approached the body and looked it over.

'All right, you can wash it now,' he said over his shoulder to his assistant, who picked up a small hand-held hose and began spraying the body with a fine mist of water while at the same time sponging off the dried blood. When he finished, Beth's body glistened under the bright lights.

The doctor began his examination with the external aspects of the body. His mortuary assistant, attired in a plastic apron, was on hand to pass the necessary instruments to the waiting hand of the elderly country doctor.

'Young female, age about....'

'Twenty-three,' offered O'Connor checking his notes.

'Yes, mid-twenties would be about right. Looks to have been a fit individual, well-nourished,' said the doctor considering the dead woman's general physique. The detectives began taking notes as the post-mortem examination proceeded.

The doctor began his formal examination by measuring and describing the throat wound. His assistant handed him a ruler.

'This won't do,' he snapped, 'give me a tape measure – something flexible.'

'Sorry doctor,' the mortuary assistant, who doubled as a general handyman, was obviously not used to proceedings of this type of post-mortem examination. He handed the doctor a flexible tape measure. The doctor bent the measure gently around the woman's neck.

'The throat wound is 11cm wide and 6.5cm deep in the fold between the chin and the upper part of the neck.' The doctor walked over to the bench near the sink and took a notebook and a pen from his pocket and rested it there. He wrote down the measurements with his hand clad in its surgical glove. Traces of blood were left on the page. The doctor walked back to the body and probed within the folds of the jagged neck wound.

'The pharynx has been completely severed just above the larynx,' he said, 'as has the right carotid artery, but not the left. Mmm, that's interesting,' the doctor murmured.

'Why?' asked O'Connor bending closer to observe the item of the doctor's interest.

'Well,' replied Dr Anderson, 'one carotid artery is situated on each side of the neck.' He indicated to the detectives their approximate location on the body. 'And when one is severed and the other one isn't, that suggests that her head has been turned or held to the side when her throat was cut.'

'Would the killer need much strength to do that, doctor?'

'Depends if the woman was struggling or not I suppose.'

The doctor continued probing, while the detectives scribbled in their note books.

'See this line along the lower border of the neck wound?' The detectives again bent forward for a closer look. 'It's intermittently jagged. That suggests multiple cuts rather than a single slash. Cutting a throat isn't as easy as you might imagine.'

McFayden shuddered inwardly.

The doctor turned his attention to the wounds on the dead woman's face. 'The upper lip shows a thick slash wound which is...' his gloved hands manipulated the tape measure, '...3cm long, extending from the mouth towards, but not reaching, the right nostril. The left corner of the mouth also has an um... 3cm slash wound running towards the angle of the jaw and there's a further slash wound under the point of the chin. It is 2.5cm long. The left front tooth has been completely knocked out.'

'By the knife blow?'

'Looks like it.'

McFayden and O'Connor exchanged glances. Seeing this kind of damage inflicted on anyone – let alone a young woman – turned their stomachs.

Dr Anderson turned his attention to the chest. 'The upper chest showed a gaping stab wound 4.5cm long in the midclavicular line, and there is a smaller gaping wound 2cm x 1.5cm, near the third rib.' The doctor's gloved hands flicked the tape measure over the wounds.

The detectives readied their pens as the doctor went on to measure and describe the 'A'. 'The right side of the 'A' shape consists of a deep slash that measures 25cm long. Two shorter and much more shallow slashes, which have not completely penetrated the skin, run parallel to the deep slash. The left side of the 'A' consists of a slash that measures 29cm long which has penetrated into subcutaneous fat. As you can see here, it's quite deep.' The doctor indicated the exposed fat and then continued once the detectives had taken a closer look.

'Three shorter, much more shallow slashes run parallel and adjacent to it. The centre bar of the 'A' consists of an 18cm horizontal slash. I've never seen anything like this.' McFayden reflected darkly to himself that the likelihood of Dr Anderson, a country hospital pathologist, seeing other bodies with huge letters of the alphabet carved into them was minimal.

Dr Anderson turned his attention to the defence wounds.

'Looks like your victim put up a bit of a fight,' he observed. Beth's body had plenty of these wounds. The doctor held up her left arm and measured the deep knife gash in her elbow. The police photographer snapped a photograph of the uplifted arm and captured on film the trickles of bloodied water running down the white surface of her skin. Also captured on film were the hands – the left hand had deep gash wounds in all the fingers and another deep wound in the web between the thumb and the index finger and the right hand had similar wounds.

Further examination revealed a small slash on Beth's left ankle. 'There's enough of these cuts,' muttered the doctor, who paused after each measurement to make a record in his note book. 'Let's hope this is the last one.'

Once Dr Anderson had described the external wounds, and they had been extensively photographed by police photographer Peter Gates, it was time to open the body to see the internal effects of these external assaults.

Using his scalpel, he opened the body from the neck down over the stomach. With a rib knife he removed the ribs and measured the length to which the knife had penetrated into vital internal organs and arteries.

'Ah,' he said, 'the right lung, the pericardium – that's the sack around the heart,' he explained for the benefit of the detectives, 'and the vena cava, have all been pierced with the long knife blade, which has entered in downwards thrusts. Your victim has bled large volumes of blood into her chest cavity. The right pleural cavity here, is completely filled with blood.'

The detectives could see for themselves without the benefit of a degree in medicine.

'Death by internal bleeding would have occurred some minutes after the upper chest wound was inflicted.'

McFayden murmured to O'Connor, 'I reckon that the chest wounds would have been the first inflicted, from what we could tell from the crime scene. Looked like she'd been attacked while she was asleep. Murderer probably got the first strike in pretty cleanly.'

'Thank God,' said O'Connor.

Dr Anderson examined other major organs which he found were all normal and free of disease.

'There's no sign of pregnancy, if that's an issue,' offered the doctor. The detectives noted this fact.

Dr Anderson then took specimens: fingernail scrapings, a lock of hair, vaginal and anal swabs, a piece of thigh muscle and 10mls of blood. He carefully labelled the specimens and handed them to the detectives. Other samples including the stomach contents and additional blood were also given to Brian Gamble, to be taken for analysis at the Forensic Science Laboratory in Melbourne.

'I don't think there's much more I can do now, you men do what you have to do.' He moved away from Beth's body to wash up and O'Connor approached the body with his fingerprint kit. He carefully prepared the ink pad and took the dead woman's cold hand in his own. He put each of her fingers awkwardly onto the black ink pad – trying to avoid knife wounds – and rolled them individually onto paper. The doctor looked curiously at this procedure and O'Connor felt compelled to explain, 'Her fingerprints are needed to differentiate between prints belonging to her at her house, and those belonging to anyone else – maybe her killer.'

The doctor nodded comprehendingly.

O'Connor finished the fingerprinting and the doctor directed the mortuary assistant, 'You can sew her up now.' The assistant gathered up the internal organs which the doctor had removed, and placed them carefully into a black plastic garbage bag and the detectives watched as he sealed the bag and put it inside the chest cavity. They knew that this routine procedure would prevent seepage from the body. The assistant then took up what looked like a large darning needle, and proceeded to sew up the post-mortem incisions.

McFayden walked over to the doctor who was removing his bloodied gown. 'What's the verdict, doctor?' he asked.

'Well, I think she was alive when the chest wounds occurred because there is evidence of extensive internal bleeding around these wounds.'

'How long would it have it taken her to die?'

'It could have taken her five minutes or so, but of course she probably would have been unconscious earlier than that.'

'How about the "A"...?'

'I can't say for certain whether she was alive then, but I think not.'

'Anything else you can add?'

'Only that prior to the attack she was a healthy young woman with every chance of living till she was 80.'

'Thanks doctor,' said McFayden, 'when can we have your written report?'

'I'll have it ready later this afternoon.'

The detectives left with their notes and their bottled specimens, to continue their investigation.

Dr Anderson meticulously finished his notes and recorded his findings in a detailed report. He put down the cause of death for the Coroner as: 'Knife wounds in chest and throat'.

His comment at the end of his report stated: 'The presence of extensive internal bleeding around the long stab wound into the chest indicates that the deceased was initially alive when this wound occurred. No similar conclusions can be made about other wounds.'

Chapter Ten
A Watery Grave?

SERGEANT GEOFF FROST HAD BEEN WITH THE VICTORIA POLICE SEARCH AND RESCUE SQUAD FOR 14 YEARS WHEN HE WAS ASKED TO COORDINATE THE SEARCH FOR THE BODY OF VIVIENNE JANICE CAMERON.

Throughout his years with the squad, Sergeant Frost had been involved in locating numerous bodies from isolated locations in Victoria. Not all of the bodies he had found had been murder victims. Indeed, many had been pulled from the wreckages of light plane crashes in the country, and located after boating accidents on Port Phillip and Westernport Bays.

Occasionally Frost and his squad were involved in the location of murder and suicide victims. One such case which stands out in his mind was that of Anton Kenny, a bikie who was connected to Melbourne's drug underworld in the 1980s, which was run by the notoriously violent criminal, Dennis Allen.

In March 1986, the Victoria Police received a tip-off from Allen himself, saying that an associate of his had killed Kenny and dumped his body in the Yarra River. Sergeant Frost maintains the best way to conduct a search is to use common sense. And so, members of the search and rescue squad consulted a Melways Street Directory and looked at the location of the murder site in Cubitt Street, Richmond, and compared it with the closest point of the Yarra River. Coupled with the common sense approach, and a good local knowledge of the Yarra and popular dumping sites along its banks and in its waters, the team were able to pin-point an area that had, in the past, yielded abandoned cars and other such stolen property.

Sure enough – after only a couple of dives in the Yarra's murky brown waters – one of Frost's frogmen discovered a 44-gallon drum on the muddy bottom. It wasn't until the drum was surfaced that they realised how gruesome the discovery was: Kenny's legs had been chain-sawed off and sealed – along with the rest of his body – into the drum with cement. Dennis Allen's mother, Kath Pettingill later told a Supreme Court jury that Allen had confessed to the murder on his death bed.

It was some six months later that Frost was given one of his more curious jobs in trying to find Vivienne Cameron. He first found out Vivienne was missing when, on the afternoon of Wednesday 24 September, 1986, he received a phone call from his good friend in the homicide squad, Detective Rory O'Connor. O'Connor told Frost that there had been an horrific murder on Phillip Island and a leading suspect's car had been found on the Island side of the San Remo Bridge.

Frost immediately told O'Connor of the difficulties entailed in the search: his squad could only search the waters surrounding the bridge for 20 minutes at a time, twice a day, when the tide would be at its lowest ebb. However, he was nonetheless confident – and he remains so today – that if Vivienne Cameron had, indeed, jumped from the bridge, there was a good possibility that he would find her. After an initial drifting period where air is expired from the body, according to Frost, the body becomes a 'dead weight' when it sinks to the bottom of a waterway. However, after an 'enzyme reaction' which coincides with decomposition – usually after it has been in the water for about four days – the body will fill with gases and float to the surface.

Geoff Frost and his divers met at the Newhaven boat ramp at 7.30 on the Thursday morning – about two days after Vivienne was presumed to have jumped from the bridge. Other police were meanwhile searching the mudflats surrounding the bridge and beaches on the island, for other evidence that might have washed up.

Sergeant Frost had brought with him from Melbourne two teams of divers – Constables Ken Hardy, Simon Ranik, Adrian Johnson and Russell Wynd – as well as two search and rescue boats.

For the next two days Frost oversaw the search of the bottom of Westernport Bay, between Phillip Island and San Remo. Metre by metre, but to no avail, Frost's divers meticulously searched the bottom. For the two days after that, knowing that if Vivienne had jumped she would have by this time floated to the top, they searched the surface of the bay.

After four days, they gave up the search. For a number of reasons Geoff Frost concluded Vivienne may not have jumped from the bridge.

When he discusses the case today, Sergeant Frost says that 'none of the signs of a suicide ritual' were present. In most of his previous cases, suicide victims had left notes and 'tidied up their affairs'.

Vivienne Cameron, he points out, had done neither. He also believes that if Vivienne had jumped from the bridge, some of her clothing or possessions – her thick-rimmed glasses, a shoe, perhaps even the floral scarf she had been wearing – would probably have been found. Frost explains exactly why his diver would have found Vivienne's body if it had been at the bottom of the bay.

Only one diver from each of the two small boats entered the water at any given time, he says. The companion diver, still on the boat, connected a long rope to his partner, who then swam out to the centre of the area under the bridge, until the rope became taut. One diver was on each side of the bridge.

Each of the divers, on different sides of the bridge, slowly swam in arcs along the bottom of the bay, keeping the guide-ropes taut behind them. They swept the bottom of the bay with their hands, ensuring that, through the murky water, they covered every centimetre.

Sergeant Frost explains that once the arc was completed, the companion of each diver pulled their partner in a full body-length to begin another arc.

Sergeant Frost said his men were searching in about 13 metres of water and visibility was poor. Nonetheless, he maintains that if there was a body at the bottom of the bay, his men would have found it.

'It just wasn't there,' Sergeant Frost says. 'We searched every centimetre, according to the correct procedure, and it just wasn't there.'

According to a Melbourne forensic pathologist, there are a number of variables when someone drowns. Water temperature, depth of the water in question and clothing worn by a person who drowns can affect whether a person will sink or float after drowning. However, a body will generally sink to the bottom, but it also may be swept along with a strong current. There have been many cases of people drowning – in both Port Phillip and Westernport Bays – and never being recovered.

Chapter Eleven

Patchwork Patterns and Awkward Silences

GILLIAN FRASER HAD LIVED ON PHILLIP ISLAND FOR EIGHT YEARS WHEN SHE RECEIVED THE MOST MEMORABLE PHONE CALL OF HER LIFE ON TUESDAY 23 SEPTEMBER.

Her good friend Paula – a nurse in the outer Melbourne suburb of Dandenong – had come to stay for the Show Day holiday and was preparing to drive the 110 kilometres back to town that night.

Unlike the rest of Victoria, Phillip Island's farmers took the public holiday on the Monday rather than the Thursday, to enable them to visit the exhibits and display their animals at the showgrounds in Flemington, without having to battle the crowds.

Gillian and Paula had been friends since they had met when they were both working at Fairfield Hospital – Gillian in the cafeteria and Paula nursing. Their friendship had begun chatting over a coffee together when Paula was on her breaks.

Paula and Gillian had both wanted a break from their present jobs and they had decided to travel to Phillip Island for a holiday. They were told, while they were there, of a local pancake business that was up for sale and decided to sublease the business. Paula and Gillian tried a few business ventures but eventually Paula returned to nursing and Gillian ran a small business in Cowes.

Like most lasting friendships, the bond between Paula and Gillian had strengthened with time and, in middle age, they got together often. Although Phillip Island was more than 110 kilometres from town, the South Gippsland Highway meant that Paula and Gillian were only a pleasant, one hour drive away from each other.

Paula arrived at Gillian's house in the afternoon of Monday 22 September, after working an early shift at the hospital. Gillian had been at work all day too. The friends enjoyed a relaxed night together catching up on what they had both been up to since they saw each other last.

It was 10 o'clock on Tuesday morning when the phone rang in the kitchen. Paula, who was elbow-deep in soapy water washing the breakfast dishes, called to Gillian, who was getting dressed, to answer the call.

'Paula, I'm so busy today – I haven't got time to chat to anyone today. Can you answer it?'

'It won't be for me – answer it yourself!'

Gillian hurried out from her bedroom and reluctantly picked up the phone: 'Hello?'

'It's Viv Cameron here, Gillian.'

'Hi Viv, you're lucky to catch me today, I'm normally at work by now but I'm hand-sewing at home today for the fashion parade,' Gillian said.

'Have you found out anything – or where to buy the patchwork house gift for Isobel?'

Gillian remembered meeting Vivienne outside the post office the week before and Vivienne had asked her where she could buy a patchwork house that she could sew for a gift. Gillian suggested that Vivienne call Dianne, whose sister made the patchwork houses.

'Do you want her number? I have it right here,' asked Gillian. 'Have you got a pencil?'

When Vivienne went silent, Gillian assumed she was writing the number down. Vivienne's side of the conversation was interrupted by voices – voices that Gillian assumed were Vivienne's two young boys talking in the background. Vivienne asked Gillian to 'hold on a sec', before she left the phone. As the background noise stopped, Gillian covered the mouthpiece and whispered to Paula that it was Vivienne on the line.

'I won't be long.' She turned her attention back to the phone as Vivienne returned.

'Boys playing up?' Gillian joked.

'It's okay now,' said Vivienne.

From her experience with dozens of phone calls over the years, Gillian knew that Vivienne was a bit awkward on the telephone. Gillian always felt it her role to make the conversation. But today she didn't have time.

'Is there anything else you want, Viv?'

'Why no...I don't think so.'

Just before hanging up, Gillian remembered the list of materials they both needed for patterns they were working on. She asked if Vivienne wanted her to read out the items on the list.

'Oh don't bother now. Bring the list with you to patchwork lessons next week and I'll get it then,' Vivienne said.

There was another one of those awkward silences that Gillian was accustomed to when speaking with Vivienne on the phone.

'Well I'd better get back to my sewing now, Viv. See you next week at class.'

'Goodbye.'

That was the last word anyone has ever acknowledged hearing from Vivienne Cameron. Gillian Fraser would be made to remember it, and the rest of their short conversation, forever.

About two hours later, Gillian and Paula went for a coffee at one of the local cafes in Cowes. It was there that they learnt that Beth Barnard had been murdered. Like the rest of the locals, Gillian was shocked. So too was Paula. Neither of the two knew Beth, but like most residents of the small community, they knew of her. Gillian was upset to hear that the young woman had been murdered, and she was vaguely concerned about her own safety – a woman living alone.

In the weeks to come, Gillian would hear much of the rumour and innuendo surrounding the dead girl and her life, but she refused to participate in the local rumour mill – having over the years developed a loathing of small town gossip. In a close-knit community like Phillip Island, the most insignificant news spread like wild fire, and so it was no surprise that the murder of the attractive young local girl spread almost instantly. The word was that Beth's throat had been cut while she lay in bed and that she'd also been stabbed three or four times. Except for the police, Ian Cairns and Donald Cameron and, of course, the killer, nobody else knew the full extent of Beth's horrific injuries. The locals would learn about the 'A' carved into Beth's chest and stomach in the 29

September edition of the *Phillip Island Sun*. Those who didn't get one delivered could pay 15 cents to read all about it.

Of course, Gillian and Paula made absolutely no connection between Beth's murder and Vivienne Cameron. That wasn't until the 6 o'clock news. Gillian was still worried at the news of Beth's murder when she turned on the television the following night to see if the crime had made the news. She was very interested when it was one of the leading items. The reporter said that police were searching for a missing Phillip Island woman, Mrs Vivienne Cameron, in connection with the savage murder of a 23-year-old farm worker, Elizabeth Katherine Barnard. Vivienne Cameron's car had been found on the Phillip Island side of the San Remo bridge, according to the news, and it was believed Vivienne had jumped from the same bridge to her death. The reporter said the car had first been seen at 5 o'clock on Tuesday morning although it wasn't positively identified by police until about 4pm the same day. It was Vivienne's sister-in-law, Pamela Cameron, who identified the car for detectives.

Gillian Fraser froze when she realised she had spoken to Vivienne some five hours after the car was first seen parked near the bridge. She was still staring at the news report when the phone rang.

'Gillian, it's Paula. Have you seen the news?'

Gillian could hardly speak: 'Yes...'

'Wasn't it Vivienne Cameron who you spoke to on the phone? How could she be jumping off the bridge at 5 o'clock Tuesday morning when you spoke to her at 10? It just doesn't make sense.'

'No. What am I going to do?'

'You've got to ring the police,' Paula told her firmly.

'No... I can't.'

'Gillian, this is vital to the police. You have to tell them now. They think Vivienne has got something to do with Beth's murder, but she can't have – not if she was talking to you on the phone about... what was it?'

'Patchwork patterns,' said Gillian, lost in thought.

'Let's face it,' said Paula, 'nobody's going to discuss patchwork if they've just killed somebody. Are they?'

'Oh my God Paula, I can't believe this.'

'You have to call the police – Vivienne could be in danger or hurt.'

Paula told Gillian that she would make the call for her. She immediately dialled the Victoria Police, D-24 emergency line, 11444. Paula briefly explained what she knew to a young constable, who said he'd pass on the information to the homicide squad.

Paula rang work and said she was taking a few days off – her boss gave her compassionate leave. Paula quickly packed a bag, grabbed her car keys and drove directly to Phillip Island. She knew that Gillian could use the support.

Detective Senior Sergeant Jack McFayden visited Gillian Fraser at her home less than an hour after Paula's phone call to the police.

McFayden, sensitive to Gillian's trauma, gently coaxed the story from her. McFayden was pleased when Paula arrived shortly after the interview began because she reinforced Gillian's story of the phone call and the time it was received. Gillian emphasised that Vivienne couldn't have jumped off the bridge and drowned before she rang her at 10am.

After carefully taking notes and checking their facts, again and again, he left Gillian and Paula to discuss the shocking turn of events.

The next night, three detectives from the homicide squad in

Melbourne visited Gillian. They too would check through her story and corroborate it with Paula. However, they were more sceptical than McFayden.

'Are you sure it wasn't on Monday that Mrs Cameron called you?' asked Detective O'Connor.

'I've told you... I'm positive because Paula wasn't even here on Monday morning and I was at work most of the day. It couldn't have been Monday,' Gillian said.

'Are you sure it was her on the phone – not someone pretending to be her?' O'Connor had to cover all bases.

'I am absolutely certain,' said Gillian. 'It couldn't have been anyone else because of what she was talking about. Nobody else would have known about the patchwork house she wanted to buy – besides, I've spoken to Vivienne enough times on the phone to recognise her voice.'

'She was normal – absolutely normal,' said Gillian, trying to emphasise her conviction to the detectives. 'I don't believe she could have done it... not the way she spoke. I just can't believe it.'

'People can just snap. People can draw a lot of strength and just snap.'

Gillian could believe that people could snap – indeed she had heard of such cases of unlikely people committing crimes. What Gillian couldn't believe was that the woman, with whom she had a completely normal conversation on Tuesday morning, could have mutilated a young woman only hours before their phone conversation.

'So you mean to say that you were talking to her on the phone... why have we had police divers searching for her body under the bridge then?'

'I don't know,' said Gillian. 'All I know is that that's when she called me. I'm certain.'

Chapter Twelve
A Farmer's Affair

FERGUS CAMERON WAS GIVEN TWO DAYS TO REGAIN HIS COMPOSURE. DETECTIVE O'CONNOR HAD ALREADY SPOKEN, ALBEIT BRIEFLY, TO FERGUS.

But it was his decision that Jack McFayden should conduct the formal interview on Thursday – two days after Beth's murder and Vivienne's disappearance.

McFayden joined the police force on the 11 January, 1965 when he was just 18 years old. During his career, he worked at Russell Street Police Headquarters in Melbourne and police stations in Richmond and St Kilda. Inner city policing opened the eyes of the young country-bred police officer to some of the harsher realities of life. McFayden was transferred to the armed robbery squad and he worked with the team that investigated one of Melbourne's most notorious crimes – six heavily armed bandits raided the Victoria Turf Club in April, 1976 and made off with 1.3 million dollars – the so-called Great Bookie Robbery. McFayden went on to work on the consorting squad and then the major crime squad, before being transferred to the first of a string of country police stations. He planned to work at the Wonthaggi CIB until he retired.

McFayden was known widely in policing circles – both personally and by reputation – as 'the most honest, hard-working cop you would ever come across'.

McFayden, who had taken thousands of statements during his 21 years in the force, knew too well that it was difficult, and often distressing, to take a statement from a person who had lost somebody close to them. He anticipated that Fergus Cameron would be no different. After all, in one day he had lost both his wife and his lover.

Early on Thursday morning, McFayden drove his unmarked police car from Wonthaggi to the Phillip Island suburb of Ventnor. Watts Road, Ventnor was home of three branches of the Cameron family. Fergus Cameron lived on the corner of Watts Road and Berry's Beach Road and Marnie Cairns, his sister, and Donald Cameron, lived further down what was little more that an unmade gravel road. McFayden headed for the home of Marnie Cairns. Fergus had been staying with his sister and her husband Ian since Monday night.

All three properties backed on to a cliff face and the wild seas of Bass Strait. The cliff face and the reef behind their properties had an infamous historical significance. In the late nineteenth century a ship from Wales, the *SS Speke*, crashed into the reef outside Watt Point, after the captain mistook a bushfire for navigation lights. The captain's attempts to save his ship had been dashed after the anchor chains broke. For several days the ship lay stranded, creaking and groaning as it was broken up on the reef as the tides changed. It sat in its watery grave until the wreck was sold for about 10 pounds. Some of the timber was used to make a barge to salvage the anchor chain and two three-tonne anchors. The ship's bell now signals the beginning of service at the Presbyterian church on the Island, while the captain's armchair had stood in the old Isle of Wight Hotel, which was burnt to the ground in 1925. Much of the salvaged timber from the *Speke* was used to build pig-sties, chook sheds, cattle barns and farm sheds. Some of them are still standing today. The figurehead of the SS *Speke*, a beautiful woman holding a bunch of daffodils, wearing a long blue dress with a white collar and cuffs, was partly salvaged and repaired by local school children under the direction of their headmaster. Today it can still be seen at the Heritage Centre in Cowes.

A sign, behind the Cameron properties, tells tourists where to look for the wreck from the cliffs. The Cameron's sheep had the run of the cliffs, which they shared with – and sometimes to the detriment of – mutton bird rookeries.

On top of the cliffs and further inland, Jack McFayden drove up the long driveway, parked his car and knocked on the front door of Marnie Cairns's house. Marnie opened the door, greeted McFayden, and quietly led him to a bedroom where Fergus, who had been mildly sedated, lay propped up in bed wearing pyjamas. McFayden immediately noticed a wound, just above Fergus's left ear lobe, that had been stitched together. Fergus looked surprisingly alert and composed.

After quickly dispensing with introductions, McFayden accepted Fergus's offer of a chair, knowing that the interview could take several hours. Little did he know that it would be dark when he left the Cairns house about 12 hours later.

McFayden couldn't help but wonder what must be going through Fergus Cameron's mind: how would you feel, he wondered, if your wife disappeared and your lover was murdered on the same night? McFayden would later say that, given Fergus Cameron's predicament, he had 'never seen anybody so cool, calm and collected'. McFayden had been told that Fergus was suffering from shock. Perhaps, he thought, the sedatives accounted for Fergus Cameron's lack of visible emotion.

The interview began much like any other: when and where were you born, where did you grow up and where did you go to school? Usually McFayden asked such questions, not only to find out about his subject, but also to put them at ease. But the detective would later reflect that Fergus Cameron didn't need to relax any further.

McFayden soon learnt that Fergus had been educated at the exclusive Scotch College in the eastern Melbourne suburb of Hawthorn where he had matriculated in 1968. After leaving school he had worked with an estate agent in Geelong, the largest rural city in Victoria. A short time later he had left his job in Geelong and returned to Phillip Island to work on the family property. Just before Christmas in 1976, aged 26, Fergus Archibald Stewart Cameron had married Vivienne Janice Candy.

Fergus told McFayden that his marriage to Vivienne had been difficult in the early years and that he and his wife had never been very good at talking their problems through. Their relationship reached its pinnacle, he said, when their two children were born: the eldest in 1978 and the second in 1981.

McFayden wrote quickly on a large note pad, balanced on his knee, while Fergus spoke. Fergus would eventually sign each page of the statement, after reading through it to make sure it was factually correct.

He calmly explained to the detective that the basis of his marital problems lay in the very different backgrounds of him and

Vivienne. Vivienne, originally from Warrnambool, had been living in Melbourne when they first met. At the time, Fergus had been living briefly in the small Western District township of Mortlake.

McFayden decided to gently steer the conversation towards the events leading up to Vivienne's disappearance and Beth's murder. He had been told that Fergus had first met Beth at the Penguin Parade on Phillip Island's south westernmost point – Summerland Beach, over which the penguins waddled to their burrows each night. He asked him about his job at the Penguin Parade.

Fergus told McFayden that he had started working part-time at the parade in December, 1978. 'I started off as a casually employed ranger and that is what I am basically now.' Given that half a million tourists – including thousands from Japan and America – came to watch this spectacle of nature each year, his job was not inconsiderable.

'Depending on the time of year, the hours of work vary but they are basically from just before dusk to about three hours on,' Fergus volunteered, '...and I'm paid for a minimum of two hours.'

Fergus first laid eyes on Beth in 1984, when he sat in on her interview after she had applied for a job at the Penguin Parade. Beth got the job as a parade ranger and her hours sometimes coincided with his. 'During this time we got to know each other but nothing personally as she had her social life and I had mine,' he said.

In April, 1985 – after they'd known each other just four months – Fergus asked Beth to work part-time with him on his farm. She also continued to work at the Penguin Parade where – perhaps because she was one of the few young women there, but not-withstanding her good looks and lively personality – a number of her young, male co-workers vied light-heartedly for her affections.

Fergus became ill with bronchitis soon after he hired Beth, leaving many of his farming duties to her. But as soon as he recovered, he began working closely with her on the farm. One night Fergus and Vivienne had even accompanied Beth and her current boyfriend to the nearby Westernport Hotel. '...I can't recall who he was,' Fergus said of the boyfriend.

'It was at this time I believe that we were pretty good mates, although at this stage it hadn't gone any further than that. Sometime in mid-May, just before the school holidays started, I was due for holidays myself from work so the staff at the Penguin Parade decided to have a party. At the party Beth asked several members to go back to her place in McFees Road in Rhyll, for a drink, but subsequently I was the only one who did,' Fergus told McFayden. He described their first sexual encounter simply: 'At her place we sat and drank and talked, made love in her bedroom and I left after a couple of hours.'

Fergus hadn't expected to see Beth again before his holidays began, but he bumped into her about four days later when he went to collect his pay from the Penguin Parade. 'I can remember being delighted to see her and she was delighted to see me,' he said.

But the holiday with Vivienne and the two boys apparently gave Fergus time to reflect on his new-found sexual relationship with Beth. So much so, that by the time he returned to work he had resolved to finish the brief affair. The relationship with Beth 'was going totally against any values I did hold'.

In light of this comment, Jack McFayden was surprised when Cameron told him that he and Beth had, a short time later, enrolled in a St Johns Ambulance course together. They had, said Cameron, taken every opportunity to see each other as much as possible. '...it was obvious that we had a loving relationship,' he said.

McFayden smiled at Cameron and considered carefully what he had just said. Thankfully, Marnie interrupted the detective and the farmer with cups of tea and sandwiches. McFayden watched Fergus eat. He was pleased that Marnie's interruption gave him a break, because his hand had begun to ache from writing down, word for word, everything Fergus was saying.

After lunch, Fergus went on to tell McFayden how he and Beth had discussed their affair, decided they were 'on the wrong track', and resolved that it should finish. 'But this wasn't a reality and we would make love on a regular basis, approximately twice weekly,' he said.

'This took place mostly at her place, although occasionally on the beach or in one of our cars.'

While Vivienne was oblivious to her husband's new sexual exploits, Beth and Fergus were not discreet enough to keep their affair a secret. Other workers at the Penguin Parade occasionally saw the pair in one of the cars. They noticed that the windows were usually fogged.

It was about this time, around July in 1985, that Vivienne told her husband that he was giving Beth favoured treatment around the farm. However, Fergus believed that his wife still didn't suspect his illicit relationship with the young farmhand.

Even before the affair began, the Cameron's marriage had been strained, according to Fergus.

'My sexual life with Vivienne was extremely quiet. I'm sure that she had feelings towards me but I found it difficult to have feelings toward her,' he explained to McFayden. 'This was the situation before I met Beth but things deteriorated between us since I met her.'

Fergus told McFayden he made another 'concerted effort' to end the affair. However, this must have been short-lived because, while Beth was on holiday for six weeks in New South Wales, Fergus said he rang her every week. After she returned to Phillip Island in October, Fergus and Beth again saw each other as often as possible – early in the morning or after he'd finished at the Penguin Parade, at her place.

But this time, Beth's stay on the island was short and, after only about 10 days, she left on a holiday to the Maldive Islands, off the coast of India, with her two closest female friends, Deborah and Margaret. Again, this presented Fergus with a reason to end the relationship. But, he told the detective that in mid-November '…she returned from her trip and the relationship continued immediately…'

Vivienne and Fergus still hadn't discussed what had become huge problems in their marriage and a growing chasm in their communications. Then, in mid-December, Vivienne caught Fergus in the shearing shed with his arm around Beth. Fergus told McFayden he couldn't exactly remember why he had his arm around Beth, suffice to say 'it was an affectionate hug, the sort of hug you would give to anyone to whom you are close'.

Vivienne asked Fergus to go back to the house with her. When he refused, the husband and wife stood in the garden. Vivienne asked Fergus if he was having an affair with Beth. 'No. We are very good mates,' he lied.

He explained to the detective that, despite Vivienne's distress and constant questions, he denied the affair with Beth who was so shaken by the event, she quit her job at the Cameron farm and also gave notice to her bosses at the Penguin Parade.

Two days before Christmas and just four days after the Cameron's wedding anniversary, the Penguin Parade workers had a party at Beth's house which lasted until the early hours. Fergus thought he might have kissed Beth at the party, but he is adamant they didn't make love that night. Just before dawn, Fergus said he slipped into bed beside Vivienne, who he presumed was sleeping. She wasn't.

'She punched me in the face to begin with and I rolled over on my stomach and she punched me on my back and she was crying, extremely distraught, wanting to know why I was so late. I said that it was a good party and after about five minutes she quietened down and I held her as tight as I could and she cried some more and I went to sleep.'

McFayden was carefully considering Fergus Cameron's side of the story. The way things were going, Fergus had freely admitted his affair with the much younger female farmhand, and at the same time portrayed his wife as a hysterical, violent woman, insane with jealousy.

McFayden had never met Vivienne Cameron. However, he pictured in his mind the image of her on the photographs that the family had released to the police. She was a plain, small woman. She had fair hair cut in a page boy style and she had been smiling awkwardly – even self-consciously – at the camera. McFayden mentally compared this apparently docile woman who wore gold-rimmed glasses with thick lenses, with the description of her state of mind on the police circular: 'DISTRESSED STATE – SUICIDAL – HOMICIDAL'.

McFayden kept writing Fergus's words: 'Beth resigned from the Penguin Parade and was all set to go to Werribee and was looking for accommodation,' Fergus said. He had not seen much of Beth during January while she was making plans to leave the Island. But a couple of days before she was due to go, Fergus and Beth sat alone together in the Penguin Parade commentary box, looking out across the sand over which the penguins would soon surf up onto the beach and toddle to their burrows.

'I told her that there was no way I wanted her to go and she told me that there was no way she wanted to go and she immediately spoke to the senior staff and she was immediately reinstated,' Fergus said. A short time later, Beth began working on the Cameron farm again.

'I was thinking that the only course open to Vivienne and myself was for us to separate but I don't think Vivienne saw it that way at all. I thought that with me and Vivienne separated, the relationship between Beth and myself could be more open. Up to this stage Vivienne didn't say anything to me about my relationship with Beth, but on a number of occasions she questioned the wisdom of having Beth working around the place.'

On a weekend in February 1986, Fergus and Vivienne went alone to Lorne, a picturesque coastal town on Victoria's Great Ocean Road, about 90 minutes' drive from Geelong. According to Fergus, they went away with the specific intention of trying to reconcile their marriage. However, they didn't discuss their problems and again, on several other occasions when they went to Melbourne together for the weekend, they failed to patch things up. This didn't surprise McFayden because, in the next sentence, Fergus explained that, at no time did his affair with Beth decrease – in fact, he said, they had become even closer. They would see each other often. He would slip over to her house early in the morning, or Beth would come over to his house for lunch when Vivienne was at work at the Community House. Fergus told McFayden that Beth was almost at the point of telling her family about the relationship.

During the shearing season Beth and Vivienne worked side by side on the farm. Such obvious tension culminated on the last day of the shearing season when all the workers, including Beth, had gone home.

'We had all been drinking, including myself, and when we'd gone up to the house, Vivienne became violent with me over Beth. She said that Beth was a scheming little bitch and in general criticising her to the point of hatred. She was very disparaging as to my admiration for Beth, but did not to my knowledge accuse me of having an affair with her but I think she assumed I was. Vivienne also said she was annoyed that Beth didn't leave and go to Werribee four months before.

'During this argument she punched me half a dozen to a dozen times around the face, arms and chest and at that time I was sitting on a stool in the back porch. I feel that she had every right to do what she was doing, not because of my association with Beth but because she deserved some answers and I wasn't giving her any. Although Vivienne was drinking on this occasion, she wasn't drunk but probably had enough to drink to say what she had wanted to say for a long while.'

McFayden reflected that this was the second time in several hours that Fergus had spoken about his wife's allegedly violent nature. He wondered too, how Fergus could have sat on that stool without falling off or protecting himself, while his wife beat him about the head.

From about May, 1986, Fergus told McFayden he had become less concerned about protecting his family. Vivienne and Fergus had discussed their marriage and its problems and Vivienne had asked him to see a marriage counsellor. Fergus had told her that he didn't see what good it would do.

Around this time, Fergus explained, Vivienne had received a five thousand dollar inheritance and she asked Fergus to quit his job at the Penguin Parade and spend more time with her and the children. Fergus said that he was 'totally opposed' to quitting his part-time job, knowing it would mean that he'd see less of Beth.

At this point Fergus interrupted himself and said, '... I forgot to include earlier, I first told her I loved her in December, 1985 and she was immediately reciprocal.' McFayden duly recorded this fact.

According to Fergus, Beth was willing to wait until the end of the year to see what happened with his marriage. However, Fergus was anticipating that he would be leaving Vivienne and the children to live on another part of the Island. He wouldn't contemplate living with Beth because, he said, it would not be fair on her family.

'It had got to the point that if I had any sexual relations with Vivienne it would have been an enormous feeling of guilt towards Beth. Although Vivienne didn't say anything, I could tell that she felt rejected and I tried to compensate by doing all the things a loving husband should do, such as making her comfortable and making her wanted and needed in other ways and I used to confer with her in everything but our own personal relationship.'

About seven weeks before Beth's murder, on a Monday morning, Fergus recalled, he was late picking up his younger son to take him to kindergarten. Fergus said Vivienne was furious and had abused him for spending his time with Beth. 'She said she had had enough.'

He recalled that Vivienne had, once again, asked him to get help to save the marriage, to which he had replied: 'Don't be stupid'. Driving her own car, Vivienne had then followed Fergus to the Phillip Island Race Track where they had another heated discussion. Asked by McFayden what it was about, Fergus said, '...I have no idea'.

McFayden thought it odd that, while Fergus could remember the time and date of the argument, he couldn't remember what was said.

Fergus described his relationship with Vivienne in the seven weeks before Beth's murder – which included Vivienne's birthday – as being 'polite and cooperative'.

Jack McFayden was relieved when Marnie Cairns again interrupted with cups of tea. It gave the detective time to think about what Fergus had said: about the arguments and the violence, about his refusal to break off the relationship and, most importantly, about the apparent anomalies in Fergus Cameron's memory.

Chapter Thirteen

The End of the Statement

WHEN JACK MCFAYDEN HAD FINISHED HIS CUP OF TEA, AND GIVEN HIS
WRITING HAND A WELL-DESERVED REST, HE TURNED HIS ATTENTION ONCE
MORE TO THE PYJAMA-CLAD FARMER PROPPED UP COMFORTABLY IN BED.

Fergus continued talking, bringing his narrative closer to the time
of Beth's murder. On the second-last night of Beth Barnard's life,
Sunday, 21 September 1986, Fergus had arrived at his lover's house
about 8pm, he told McFayden.

Fergus recalled that Beth was 'despondent' because she had
been struck with a sinus infection and Dr Paul Flood – who two
days later would identify her mutilated body – had put her on
antibiotics.

Beth was also depressed because she could see no change in
her relationship with Fergus. Although Beth was unwell and

Fergus only stayed with her for less than an hour, he later told detectives that he and Beth had made love during that time. Fergus told McFayden he arrived home to his wife shortly after 9pm – after a 10 minute drive – where he answered a number of phone calls until after midnight. By 8.30 on Monday morning, he was back at Beth's house. He told the detective that he had noted no change in her mood and as he left, he had promised her he would ring her at lunch time. '...she was a lot more cheerful and was keen for me to see her after the penguins on Monday night, which I did.'

After finishing work about 8pm, Fergus said he drove his 1978 Holden sedan to Beth's house, where she met him at the back door. Consistent with the statement of Beth's next door neighbour, Dianne, Fergus said he drove his car up the driveway with the head-lights on and parked it in the backyard between a gum tree and the garage. Only Dianne said she saw a car at 7.50pm, not after 8pm.

After Beth met Fergus at the door, he noticed that the security door hadn't been locked. '...I told her to be more security conscious and keep the door locked,' he told McFayden, who nodded at the irony.

During his visit, Fergus had sat in a beanbag in the lounge room and discussed with Beth, among other things, his marriage to Vivienne. 'We were both more optimistic than we had been for a while about Vivienne and myself separating. There was no reason but we were just both optimistic.'

Fergus Cameron told Jack McFayden he left Beth's house about 9.05pm. While they had 'kissed and cuddled' each other, he was adamant that they did not 'make love' that night. 'When I have said I made love to Beth I am referring to sexual intercourse but I don't like using that term,' he explained to the detective.

Before Fergus went home to his wife, Beth told him that she

Above: Beth Barnard in the Maldive Islands, Indian Ocean, in the last year of her life

Below: The Barnard farmhouse, where Beth lived and the scene of her murder

Above: The Barnard farmhouse from the side driveway

Left: Vivienne Cameron. Police used this photograph after her disappearance

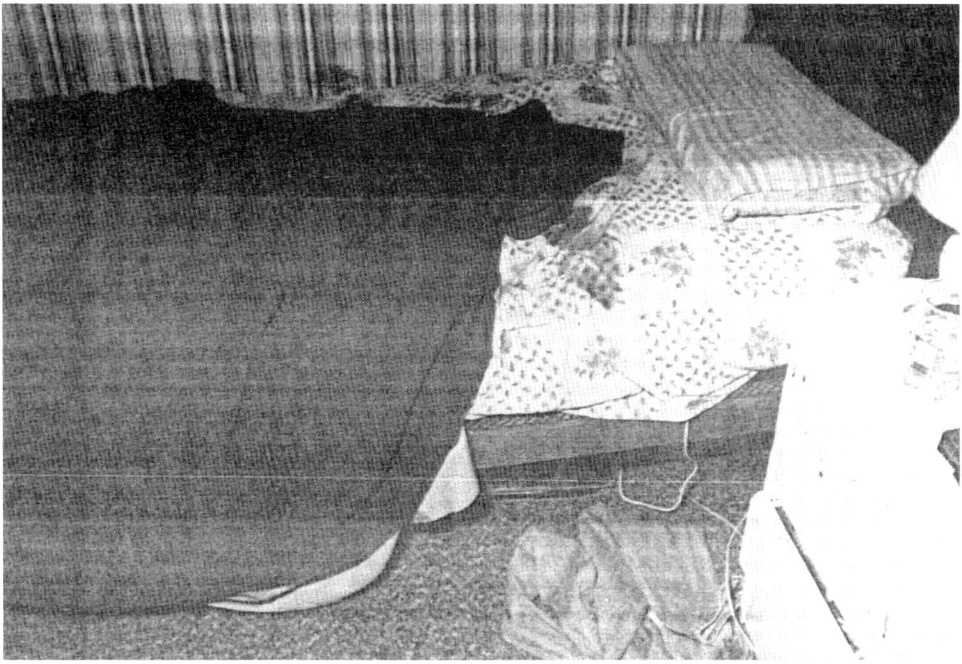

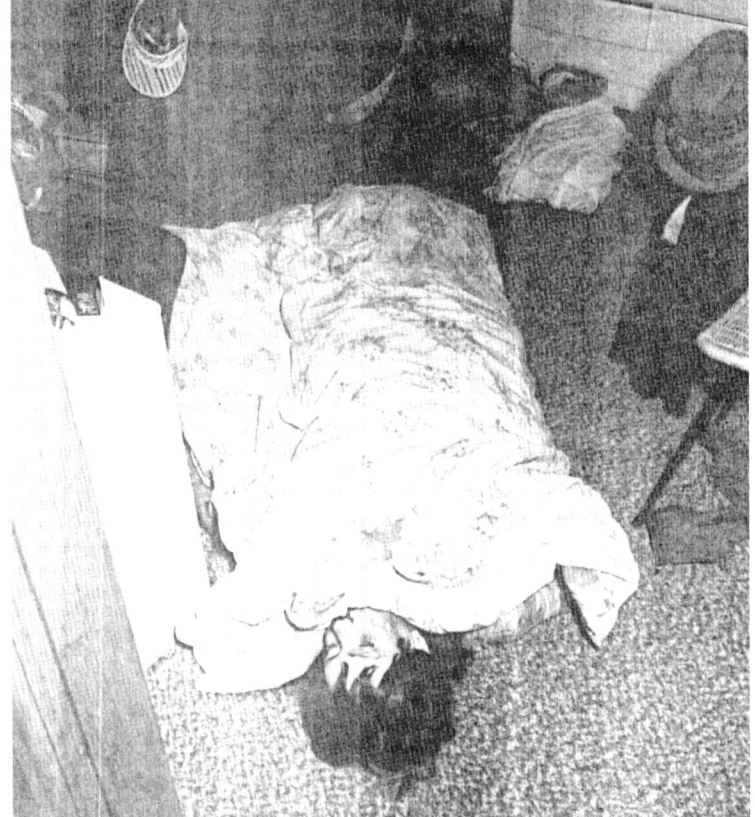

Above: The bloodstained bed in which Beth Barnard was attacked

Crime scene photographs

Left: Beth's body and quilt, arranged in the manner in which police found them

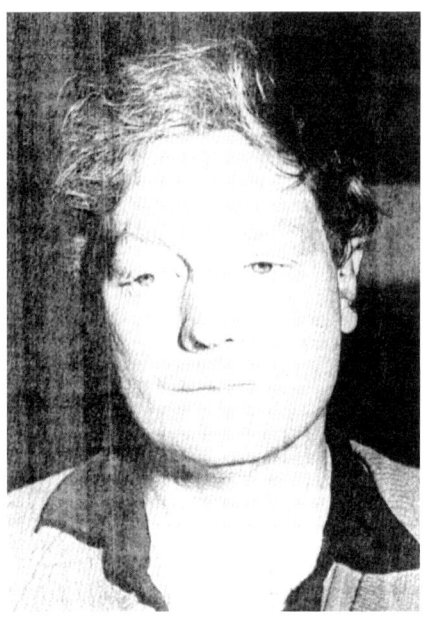

Above: Fergus Cameron, stitches visible in left ear

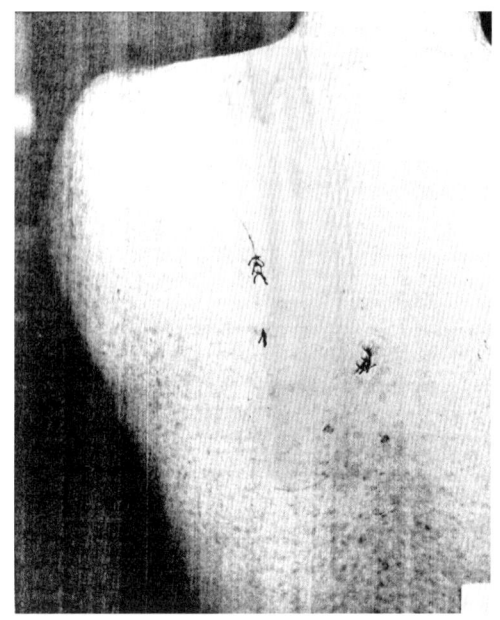

Above: Wounds and stitches to Fergus Cameron's back

Police photographs

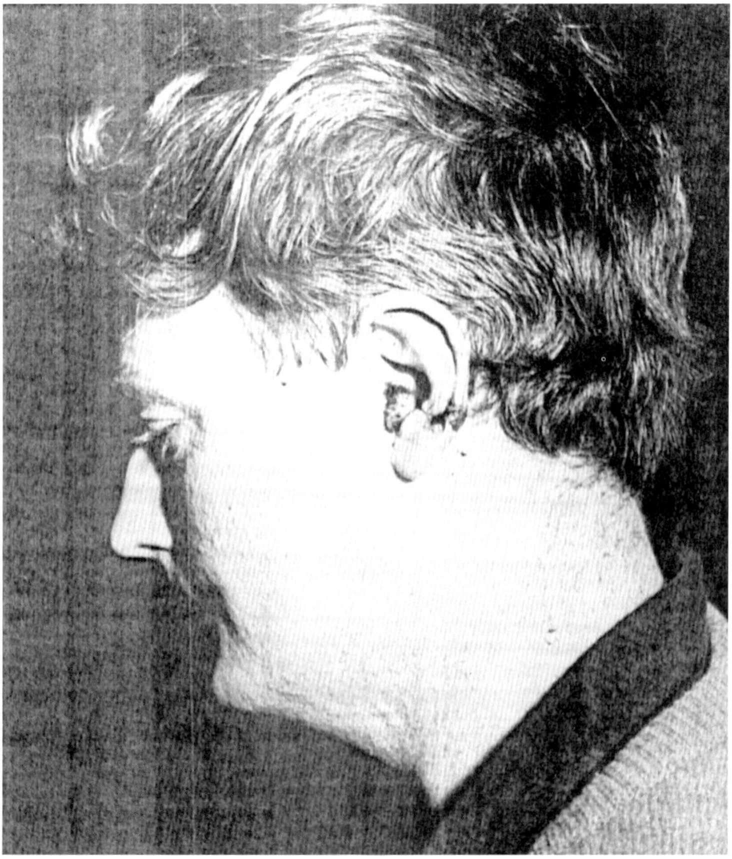

Left: Ear wound and stitches

Left: Det Alan (Jack) McFayden conducted the major interviews in the Barnard case

Below left: Det Rory O'Connor of the Homicide squad examines the Barnard file at his Russell Street offices in Melbourne

Below right; Crime scene examiner, Brian Gamble, police forensic laboratory, now a sergeant

Above: Search and rescue squad officers of the Victoria Police, Sgt Geoff Frost (left) and Simon Ranik

Sgt Geoff Frost coordinated the search of Westernport Bay for the body of Vivienne Cameron

Above: The Cowes Community House where Vivienne worked

Below: The arrow points to the spot where the Cameron's Land Cruiser was found, near the San Remo–Phillip Island bridge

The San Remo–Phillip Island bridge. The Coroner found that Vivienne Cameron jumped from this bridge to her death in the waters below – her body was not recovered

was thinking of driving back to Melbourne that night or early the next day. Sitting in the bedroom at Marnie's house and carefully writing down Fergus's statement, McFayden couldn't help but wonder if Beth would still be alive had she made that drive to her parents' home.

'I thought that she would stay overnight and go the following morning as I told her I would come around then and we never missed a chance to see each other,' Fergus said. McFayden asked if Fergus happened to remember what Beth had been wearing when he left her house that night. Most people, especially men, were notoriously bad at remembering details of women's clothing. To his surprise, Fergus recalled exactly what Beth had on.

'...she was wearing a woollen jumper but I don't remember the colour, and shirt, bra and light blue tracksuit trousers... on her right wrist she was wearing a silver band bracelet and a chain bracelet which was a gift from me.' Forensic photographs later showed this exact ensemble laid out on the second single bed in Beth's bedroom.

Fergus paused and then added, 'When I left Beth on Monday night this was the last time I saw her alive.'

McFayden asked Fergus whether Beth locked her door after he left. 'When I left she walked with me to the car and kissed me goodbye so I am unable to say if she locked the door or not but I think she would have.'

Fergus told the detective he turned left into McFees Road and headed for his home. When he arrived, his sister Marnie was sitting at the kitchen table and his sons were asleep. He immediately noticed that Marnie was 'very agitated' and Vivienne was 'visibly trembling'. Fergus was saved by the ring of the telephone. As he spoke for 15 or 20 minutes, he noticed that Vivienne was drinking a glass of wine. '...I could see that Vivienne was very upset but not showing it to Marnie.' McFayden wondered how Vivienne could be 'visibly trembling' and 'very upset' and 'not show it to Marnie'.

Fergus said that after the phone call Marnie told him that she had rung the Penguin Parade at eight o'clock, only to be told that he had already left for the night. The drive home should have taken 10 minutes and the two women had been waiting for him for over an hour and a half. Fergus, it seemed had been caught out. Realising that she had chosen a bad time to visit, Marnie left almost immediately, Fergus said. McFayden was again struck by the lack of emotion in Fergus's recounting of the events leading up to the death of his lover and the disappearance of his wife. He wondered again if it was the tranquillisers.

According to his statement, Fergus shut the back door after his sister left, walked back to the dining room and picked up his glass of wine. Vivienne followed him and screamed, 'Where have you been?'

'I just said, "I've been talking to Beth". She then raced at me with the glass of wine and screamed, "I knew you were with the little bitch". I think she hit me with the wineglass which broke on the left side of my head and cut my left ear. I turned my back away from her and she hit me two or three times with the broken glass.'

Fergus said he had been standing in the doorway between his dining room and the hall. He then turned and walked to a bedroom at the top of the house, where he sat on the bed. A significant amount of blood was later found on the bed. However, forensic tests later showed it to be Vivienne's Type A blood – not Fergus's Type O, PGM 2-1 – spattered around the room.

He told McFayden that Vivienne had followed him to the bedroom. 'She was screaming out things including, "I knew what was going on. I've been watching the number of hours you've been working. I suppose everyone out there knew what was going on". She said a lot of other things but I can't remember what they were.'

Fergus told McFayden that his wife's rage had lasted for no more than 90 seconds and had quickly changed to concern, '...as there was blood everywhere and she wanted to take me to hospital immediately'. However, forensic tests would later show that Fergus's blood was only found on the shirt he had been wearing, on a pink tissue in his bathroom and on a blue pullover belonging to Vivienne – but McFayden didn't know that yet.

'At that point I went and poured myself a whisky and Vivienne kept insisting that I go to hospital.'

McFayden asked Fergus if he had defended himself during the attack, to which he replied: 'Vivienne was not injured at all and at no time was she struck.' Fergus told McFayden that a short time later he and his wife were holding each other and crying. He finally agreed to go to hospital, but only after his sister Marnie was asked by phone – around 10.15pm – to come over to mind the boys.

Vivienne and Fergus had left before Marnie arrived to look after the young boys, who had apparently slept through the violent fight and their mother's screaming. Fergus said that as Vivienne drove the Holden sedan with him beside her in the passenger seat, she had again told him that she had known what had been going on between her husband and Beth. '...the conversation was fairly calm until we got to the hospital... As she was turning off the ignition she turned to me and said, "I'm just going to get the little bitch".'

Fergus told McFayden he hadn't taken his wife's threat towards Beth seriously. '... I thought that her physical anger had been vented on me and the subsequent concern would stop her doing any more acts of violence.

'While we were waiting for the doctor, Vivienne said to me, "Beth is obviously very special to you Fergus", and I replied, "Yes she is",' Fergus said in the interview. 'She then said something similar to, "I didn't mean what I said before". I took this to mean that she didn't have any intention of doing any harm to Beth.'

According to Fergus, Vivienne had insisted that he stay at the hospital overnight, but he had refused and the doctor had also thought this unnecessary. They arrived home about midnight, he said, to be met by Marnie who had been keen to get home herself. According to Fergus, both he and Vivienne had wanted Marnie to stay and talk to them. 'Marnie still believed that there was still time to have marriage counselling but Vivienne and I didn't. It was agreed that I should spend the next couple of nights at Marnie's place.' Fergus said he was the only one who opposed this suggestion.

After Marnie left, Fergus said he and Vivienne – who several hours earlier had been embroiled in a violent argument – had joked that the hospital apparently had little concern for his safety. For the next 90 minutes, he and Vivienne talked about their problems, Fergus told McFayden.

'...the following suggestions all came from Vivienne: that we separate immediately, that she resign from her job and move to Melbourne [and] that I have custody of our children. I agreed to this and she said that I was an excellent father. She wasn't a very good mother and I disagreed and she gave me two warnings, one was not to be too stern with the children, and not to take it for granted that Beth was going to make an excellent mother.

'She helped me pack a bag and talked about what I would need the next couple of days and I said that I would give her a ring in the morning to see how she was getting on and she drove down to Marnie's. At Marnie's place we sat in our car, which was the

Holden sedan 1978 model, and held each other and I said to Vivienne who was driving, "I wish we had done it differently". She said, "I'll give it a good bash but I don't think I'll make a very good divorcee."

'I then said goodbye to Vivienne, and Marnie kissed her goodnight and Vivienne left in our Holden sedan and I haven't seen her since.'

About 8.30 on Tuesday morning – some seven hours after Vivienne dropped Fergus at his sister's house – he said he took a phone call from his sister-in-law Pam Cameron. According to Fergus, Pam told him that at 3.30am – just five hours earlier – Robyn Dixon had picked up his children after receiving a phone call from Vivienne.

'My anxiety was further increased when I was told that Vivienne had taken the Land Cruiser, which was parked in the shearing shed. On hearing the Land Cruiser, Beth would automatically think it was me and open the door. The two people who drove the Land Cruiser were either Beth or myself.'

Finally, Fergus Cameron told Jack McFayden that, to the best of his knowledge, the rear outside light at Beth's place was always left on but she usually slept with the inside lights turned off.

It was almost 10pm when Fergus signed his statement, over 12 hours after McFayden had started interviewing him. McFayden took the 25 handwritten pages with him. He would type them up the next day and Fergus would sign the typed copy later.

It wasn't McFayden's job at this stage to question Fergus – merely to take his statement – whatever it might be. The questioning would come later.

Chapter Fourteen

Forensic Drive, Macleod

On 16 October and 24 October 1986 – around a month after Beth's murder – Dr Bentley Atchison, then a scientific officer with the Victoria Police State Forensic Science Laboratory, situated in the aptly named Forensic Drive in Macleod, received four sealed plastic bags.

Two of the bags, he noted, were labelled 'O'Connor' and the remaining two had the name 'Gamble' on them.

As a forensic scientist, it was Dr Atchison's job to analyse items collected at crime scenes throughout Victoria for blood and other tell-tale evidence which may help police to catch perpetrators. After any murder in Victoria, the crime scene officer – in the case of Beth Barnard, Brian Gamble, a police officer specialising in the collection of forensic evidence – outlines the details of the crime for the forensic scientist.

Dr Atchison could be described as the stereotypical scientist: demure and polite, with a penchant for detail in his conversation and notes. His descriptions are articulate and methodical. His memory six years – and hundreds of cases – after first examining the Barnard-Cameron evidence – was astoundingly reliable.

In the case of any murder, the forensic scientist is given an hypothesis by the police – a scenario which usually involves key suspects – and looks for evidence to contradict it.

'The scientist doesn't act blindly. It's not just "brown matter – analyse it". The scientist works from an hypothesis,' says Dr Atchison. 'Essentially the scientist is looking for something which contradicts that hypothesis.'

In the plastic bags were: brown matter labelled 'blood scraping', grey matter labelled 'control' [both samples taken from the concrete path outside Beth's house], a continental quilt cover, a wooden-handled knife, a pillow case, a pair of jeans labelled 'Replay', a blue blanket, a bed sheet, brown matter [blood] labelled 'chest of drawers', brown matter [blood] in a plastic bag labelled 'S wall', a tap knob, a maroon towel, two cigarette packets and a box of matches, three knives from the drainer in Beth's kitchen, a face washer, three cigarette butts, a handbag and a knife from the Camerons' Land Cruiser, brown matter [blood] from the Camerons' spare bedroom, two sheets of paper from Camerons' spare bedroom, brown matter [blood] labelled 'door', brown matter [blood] labelled 'wall' from the Camerons' hallway, a sponge and a knife with a white handle, brown matter [blood] labelled 'b/room floor' from the Camerons' bathroom floor, pieces of pink tissue paper, brown matter [blood] in a plastic bag labelled 'laundry', a blue shirt belonging to Fergus Cameron, brown matter [blood] from the seat in the Camerons' Holden, a pair of blue and white underpants and a pink nightshirt worn by Beth at the time of her murder, a maroon towel and a tap knob from Beth's bathroom, samples of Beth's blood, hair, nails and muscle tissue in separate containers labelled 'Barnard', two swab sticks labelled 'perianal' and 'anal', two swab sticks labelled 'vaginal internal' and 'vaginal external', scrapings from beneath Beth's fingernails, a pair of jeans labelled 'JAB' a pair of blue panties, a brassiere and a pair of socks, a pale blue pullover labelled 'La Chic', a blue 'Cherrylane' pullover, a blue skivvy, a yellow pullover, a green pullover, a jacket and a tube of Fergus Cameron's blood. Fifty-three items in all.

Part of Bentley Atchison's job was to work out which blood belonged to each of the three people who were known, or thought, to have bled at the time surrounding Beth's murder.

There are essentially four ABO blood groups – groups A, B, O and AB, according to *Science Against Crime*, an American textbook on forensic science. Through analysing polymorphic enzymes present in blood, further sub-groups of the four main blood types can be identified. These further sub-groups of the four blood types are known as the PGM [Phosphoglucomutase] types.

In pre-DNA days, it was written: 'We can see that the more grouping systems that can be applied to a spot of blood the more the scientist can discriminate between that blood and the blood from somebody else selected at random.' (*Science Against Crime*, 1982)

Dr Atchison found, by analysing the containers of blood that he had received, that Beth's ABO blood group was Type O, PGM 1 and Fergus's was Type O, PGM 2-1. He had no sample of Vivienne's blood to analyse, but according to hospital records from when Vivienne gave birth to her two sons, he knew her blood group to be Type A. Dr Atchison was unaware of her PGM sub-group.

Nonetheless, Dr Atchison realised that because the three people had different blood types, it was easy for him to determine who had bled where.

According to the forensic evidence collected by Gamble and O'Connor, the only place Atchison found Beth had bled was at her house. Predictably, because she had bled so profusely, the scientist found her type blood on the quilt cover and other bed clothes, the jeans labelled 'Replay', on the chest of drawers near the bed in which she slept and on the blue and white underpants she had been wearing when she was murdered. He also found her blood type on two pieces of paper.

Curiously, although Atchison was able to determine that both Beth's pink nightshirt and the knife found near her body had Type O blood on them, he was unable to determine the PGM sub grouping on either item. According to his report: 'There were ABO group O human bloodstains on the blade of the wooden-handled knife, in the brown matter in the plastic bag labelled 'wall' [scrapings taken from a bloodied hand print on the wall above Beth's bed], and on the pink shirt. The PGM type/s of these stains could not be determined.'

Blood examined to be Type A, which could have been Vivienne's blood [along with 38 per cent of the population who also have Type A blood], was found on a maroon towel from Beth's bathroom, the path outside Beth's house, a cigarette packet and the match box found in the Cameron's Land Cruiser and a face washer also found in the Land Cruiser. Dr Atchison also found Type A blood in the scrapings taken from the spare bedroom at the Cameron's house and from their laundry.

A number of items of clothing taken from the Cameron's house also tested positive for Type A blood, including the 'La Chic' pullover, the blue skivvy, the yellow pullover, the green pullover, and the blue 'Cherrylane' pullover. It was obvious that if this blood did indeed belong to Vivienne Cameron, she too had bled a great deal. Vivienne wasn't wearing any of these items of clothing when she took Fergus to the hospital. The clothes she was wearing, a pink mohair jumper, blue jeans and a floral scarf, were never found and presumably Vivienne was still wearing them when she disappeared.

Dr Atchison's tests found that Fergus Cameron's Type O, PGM 2-1 blood was present on only three items: pink tissues found in his bathroom, the blue shirt he had been wearing when Vivienne allegedly attacked him with a wineglass and the blue 'Cherrylane' pullover.

On a white card, Dr Atchison sketched the 'Cherrylane' pullover that was found behind the door of the Cameron's bedroom. There were two blood types discernible: Type A and Fergus Cameron's Type O, PGM 2-1. Of the six bloodstains of the jumper, two were type A and four were Type O, PGM 2-1.

A substantial amount of Fergus Cameron's blood was also found on the blue shirt he was wearing when Vivienne allegedly attacked him with a wineglass, cutting his left ear which required stitches as did three small cuts on his back.

Once again, Dr Atchison meticulously sketched Fergus Cameron's shirt and the positioning of the bloodstains, indicated by a red marker pen. According to Atchison's diagram, the left collar, shoulder and back of the shirt bore heavy stains of Type O blood, however, only the collar had PGM 2-1 to indicate the blood was definitely Fergus Cameron's. Heavy type O bloodstaining on both front panels of the shirt could not be sub-grouped. Dr Atchison also measured, recorded and sketched the three jagged cuts in the back of the blue shirt, consistent with Fergus's injuries.

Dr Atchison's drawing of the nightshirt worn by Beth Barnard is almost completely coloured in by the red marking pen. The sketch indicates seven cuts in the material of the shirt – six in the front and one in the back. 'I thought some of the cuts [on the front of the shirt] were unusual. There were two holes [close together], a longer one and then a shorter one, with a small gap in between,' Dr Atchison says.

'I asked the experts. They didn't really know. They thought it was a fishing knife. You had the double hole which you can start thinking of all sorts of knives... it penetrates making two holes. But other people who are much more experienced than I am said that you can get a hit with a knife and another sort of jab... it really didn't go anywhere. As far as I recall, I had problems saying that knife [the one found near the body] caused that sort of [double] hole.'

In the Holden that Fergus had driven to Beth's house in the hours before she was murdered – the same car Vivienne later drove Fergus to hospital in after she had allegedly cut his left ear and the left side of his back with the broken glass – a smear of blood was found on the right hand side of the passenger seat. Other than determining that it was of human origin, Dr Atchison was not able to group this blood.

During the post-mortem examination when the fingernail scrapings were taken, the pathologist, Dr Anderson, had noted that 'scrapings from beneath all fingernails [were] negligible as the nails were clipped unusually short'. It was not surprising then, that there was insufficient blood under the nails for Dr Atchison to type.

Dr Atchison also analysed the vaginal and anal swabs by putting the specimens under his microscope. He found sperm to be present on both the internal and external vaginal swabs. His notes indicate that the sperm was 'rare'. He later explained this could indicate either a low sperm count or that sexual intercourse hadn't been recent.

'Vaginal external – which I take to mean vulval – is normally washed off in the shower or in the normal course of the day. I'd be surprised if you still found it there after two days,' Dr Atchison says.

Both the anal swabs tested negative for sperm.

Fergus Cameron said he had 'made love' with Beth on the Sunday night before her death in the early hours of Tuesday morning.

Close friends of Beth attest to her personal hygiene. They say she would have showered on Monday morning.

Unfortunately, the use of DNA [deoxyribonucleic acid] was not available for use in Australia in 1986. While the method of isolating individual genetic material within the DNA molecule was developed by geneticist Alec Jeffreys at Leicester University in 1984, its application within the realms of criminal detection didn't occur until 1987.

If Dr Bentley Atchison did have access to the use of DNA testing in the Barnard murder investigation, he may have used the technology to test the Type A blood found at Beth's house. Even if the scientific officer did not have Vivienne Cameron's blood to compare with the samples found at the Barnard house, he could have taken blood samples from Vivienne's children or her surviving parent and compared it with the samples found. The scientific officer would have been able to draw conclusions with more certainty than merely saying 'the blood could have come from any member of the 38 per cent of the community with Type A blood'.

DNA testing would have proven positively whether the semen samples came from Fergus Cameron. A negative result would have told detectives that someone else had had sexual intercourse with Beth after Sunday night. However, because this technology wasn't available, the results couldn't be more specific.

Chapter Fifteen
Marnie and Ian

In the middle of the afternoon on Thursday 25 September, while Jack McFayden was questioning her younger brother Fergus in her spare bedroom, Marnie Cairns and her husband Ian received a visit from the Melbourne homicide squad detectives, Garry Hunter and Rory O'Connor.

Hunter and O'Connor wanted to know their versions of the events leading up to the murder of Elizabeth Barnard. As was standard practice in such investigations, the couple was separated for the interview – Hunter interviewed Marnie while O'Connor spoke with her husband in a different room of their house.

Marnie Cairns began by stating her full name, address and occupation for Hunter's records. By coincidence, Marnie worked part time at Warley Hospital in Cowes – the same hospital Vivienne had taken Fergus to on the previous Monday night after she had allegedly attacked him with the wineglass.

Marnie explained the family business to Detective Hunter: she, her husband Ian, and Pamela, Donald, Vivienne and Fergus, all operated a farm in Watts Road. She explained that they all lived in separate farmhouses situated close to one another in Watts Road, Ventnor.

When Hunter asked Marnie about Beth Barnard, Marnie explained that while all the men – Fergus, Ian and Donald – worked on the farm, they had also employed a full-time farmhand – Beth Barnard.

She explained to the detective that Fergus and Beth also worked part-time at the Phillip Island Penguin Parade.

Marnie talked about how her relationship with her sister-in-law, Vivienne, had started to strengthen in the year before her disappearance. 'I would normally only see Vivienne and Pamela at family functions or when they would drop in from time to time. We all had part-time jobs during the week,' she said.

'In about May this year, Vivienne and I decided to go out for lunch on a week day that we both had off and also decided to see more of each other. This resulted after we had met for a cup of coffee shortly after the shearing had finished in April. As a result, we did see more of each other and Vivienne confided in me about different matters.'

One of the 'matters' which Vivienne spoke about with candour to Marnie was her concern about Fergus and the long hours he had been working both at the Penguin Parade and on the farm. According to Marnie, it had been during lunch in early June of 1986, that Vivienne had first broached the sensitive subject of Fergus and Beth. '... she told me she was concerned about Fergus and Beth. I said, "What, her adulation for him?" and she replied, "I think it's mutual." I told her not to be concerned because it was probably only the long hours that they worked together on the property and at the Penguin Parade.

'She said that she had noticed the way that they looked at each other and that it was more than just their working together. We spoke together for some time about this and she stated that it had caused her so much anxiety at one stage, that in desperation she had rung "Life Line" [an anonymous telephone service for people in need of support]. She was concerned about the relationship between her and Fergus, and Fergus and Beth, and felt that he had fallen out of love with her. I then strongly suggested that they seek some counselling and she doubted that Fergus would agree.'

Because Vivienne suspected that her husband was having an affair with the farm hand, Vivienne confided to Marnie during lunch that day that she could no longer feel the same way about Beth as the rest of the family did. Marnie then told Hunter that 'we all liked her [Beth], she was a hard worker, enthusiastic and bright and very good with the children'.

According to Marnie, Vivienne was uncharacteristically bitter about the suspected affair. Nonetheless, Vivienne had volunteered: '...if it wasn't Beth, it probably would have been someone else.'

Marnie told Hunter that during the next few weeks Vivienne had confided that she 'thought things between her and Fergus were improving and that they had spoken' – presumably about their marriage.

Because Vivienne had shared her suspicions with her sister-in-law, Marnie too began watching for signs of an affair between her brother Fergus, and Beth. In light of Vivienne's confidences, Marnie began taking a keen interest in the way Beth looked at Fergus while the family was lamb marking on the farm. However, Beth obviously went to some lengths to hide affections for her lover because Marnie concluded there was no difference between the looks Beth gave Fergus and anybody else working on the farm.

Once he was clear about the background of the family and its relationship with the murdered woman, Hunter led Marnie into her description of the events of the day preceding the murder of Beth Barnard – Monday 22 September, 1986.

Marnie told Hunter that, about 8.15pm on Monday, she had telephoned her brother's house to be told by Vivienne that Fergus hadn't arrived home from work at the Penguin Parade. Marnie then telephoned the Penguin Parade and was told that Fergus had already left. She decided to make the short drive along Watts Road where she would wait with Vivienne until her brother arrived home. She explained to Hunter that she had some business matters to discuss with Fergus.

Marnie arrived at Vivienne and Fergus's house around 8.30pm and, because Fergus still wasn't home, she sat and talked with Vivienne for about 30 minutes until Fergus arrived. According to Marnie, as soon as Fergus arrived home, he received a phone call almost immediately and spoke at length to a business associate.

'It was at this time that Vivienne said to stay and have a glass of wine because Fergus would be some time. I stayed and had a glass of wine and Vivienne continued to drink the one she had. I didn't see her fill it up again.'

After Fergus finished his telephone call, Marnie spoke to him briefly before going home about 9.45pm or 9.50pm.

Marnie explained to Hunter: 'I hadn't been home very long, in fact I still had my jacket on, and I received a phone call from Vivienne. She asked if I could go back and look after the children as Fergus required a couple of stitches. I could tell by the tone of her voice that there must have been some form of altercation which was probably due to his late arrival home from the Penguin Parade or even the lengthy phone call. I didn't actually ask her what had happened, but I said I would look after the children.

'I then went straight back and Ian said he would follow me. When I arrived, I checked the two boys who appeared to be asleep, and noticed that the small fan heater had been tipped over.'

Marnie told Hunter that she had then checked the rest of the house. 'I went into the toilet and noticed a pile of bloodsoaked clothing consisting of a singlet, T-shirt, a pale blue shirt from the Penguin Parade, a face washer and a towel. There were also some tissues in the basin which had blood on them. Ian arrived shortly after and I showed him the clothing. He suggested that we leave it where it was and not touch it.

'I had a look around the house and saw blood on the bed in the spare room and also on the bench in the kitchen.'

After later analysis, the blood in the kitchen and in the spare bedroom was found to be Type A blood – the same as Vivienne Cameron's.

Mrs Cairns told detective Hunter that Vivienne had later telephoned from the hospital to tell her that Fergus was receiving stitches in his back and in his ear. Vivienne told Marnie that she thought Fergus should stay in hospital overnight. After the telephone call, Marnie and Ian discovered broken glass on the dining room floor of Vivienne and Fergus's house. They also noticed a glass of Scotch and a glass of claret.

'When I was with Vivienne earlier,' Marnie said, 'we drank white wine.'

After the telephone call from Vivienne, Marnie assured Ian that she would be all right on her own until Vivienne and Fergus arrived home from the hospital. Ian left, returning to their home. Marnie told Hunter that Vivienne and Fergus had arrived home around midnight and assured her that everything was all right.

'Vivienne said that although Fergus had not stayed in the hospital, she felt that he needed a rest away from the phone and that he would not be able to work for a while. I then suggested that Fergus stay with us overnight as he had to see the doctor again in the morning. We then talked for a while and they agreed to resolve something about their future and told me not to worry, that they were okay. I went home and Vivienne said she would drop Fergus over after they had spoken.'

Vivienne and Fergus had arrived at Marnie's house around 2am. Marnie told Detective Hunter that she had given Vivienne two Mogadon tablets in an envelope and told her to take one. Vivienne had assured Marnie that she was fine.

Vivienne hadn't entered the house, choosing instead to speak with Marnie at the back door. After his wife had left, Fergus spoke candidly to his sister. She repeated his words for Hunter's benefit. '[He] said, "Well, it's all over Marnie," and was very upset. He told me that they had had a long, rational talk and Viv seemed determined that that was the only solution. We spoke very broadly and went to bed at about 3am.'

Asked about the events of the following morning, Marnie told Hunter that she had gone in to see Fergus about 7am – before she started work – and suggested he ring Vivienne and the local doctor to arrange an appointment. Marnie left for work shortly after 7.30am.

'At about 9.30am, I received a phone call at work from Fergus telling me that Vivienne had phoned Robyn Dixon at about 3.15am and asked her to look after the children as they were by themselves in the house, and that he [Fergus] was concerned about Beth. He then asked me to ring her number and let her know. I phoned Beth but there was no answer so I then rang Fergus back and told him.

'He was obviously very concerned and worried, and asked me to come home. I then arranged this with the matron ... I drove straight home and found Fergus sitting at the kitchen table looking out the window. He said, "I know something terrible's happened," or words to that effect. We waited, and I kept trying the Barnard's number but there was no answer. Fergus told me that he had asked Donald and Ian to go over and see if Beth was all right.'

It is not clear from the statements of Fergus, Marnie Cairns and other witnesses if Fergus had himself tried to ring Beth – or, for that matter, why Fergus interrupted Marnie at work to try and ring Beth at 9.30am when, around 9am, he'd sent Don and Ian to Beth's house. It is also not clear from police statements where Vivienne and Fergus's five-year-old son was during this time. Donald Cameron had picked him up from Robyn Dixon after her phone call at 7.45am because she was in a hurry to get to work. Just before 9am, Donald and Ian left for Beth's house. Marnie and Pam had both gone to work, and Fergus, in his statement, makes no mention of where his younger son was during this time.

Still receiving no reply from the Barnard house, Marnie had phoned Dr Paul Flood at the Newhaven Surgery. The doctor told Marnie that he had received a phone call from a police officer, Peter McHenry who, in the company of Ian Cairns, was on his way over to see Fergus.

'They arrived a short time later and Doctor Flood told us that Beth was dead. Doctor Flood took Fergus aside and spent some time with him.'

As Marnie told her story to Hunter, he duly scribbled her words onto a note pad. When she had finished, he asked her if she had anything else to add, to which Marnie replied: 'Just prior to leaving Viv and Fergus after they had arrived home from the hospital, I saw the broken, jagged base of a glass under a chair in the corner of the family room. I then picked it up and put it in the bin.'

This was the last time that the glass – allegedly the weapon

Vivienne chose to use on her husband – was seen. According to Brian Gamble, the Victoria Police crime scene officer who collected all evidence connected with the Barnard case, a search of the Camerons' house did not reveal the broken wineglass.

Marnie signed her statement at 4.20pm.

In a nearby room Ian Cairns was being interviewed by Senior Detective Rory O'Connor. He had no problems recalling the events surrounding the murder of Beth Barnard.

He began by explaining how Beth had come to work on the family farm. 'Elizabeth, who we all call Beth, started working for us approximately 18 months ago and helped us in all farm duties and, in particular, the handling of the stock,' he said.

'My brother-in-law, Fergus Cameron, and Beth had known each other for some years prior to her employment on the farm as they had both worked as Rangers and were still employed in that capacity. These were evening duties at the Phillip Island Penguin Parade. Beth worked with all members of the family but worked closer with Fergus as he was responsible for management of the stock. This didn't mean that they worked continuously together all day. It usually involved Fergus taking Beth to the hay storage and loading the truck. Beth would then continue around the farm whilst Fergus would continue with some other aspect.'

Unlike his wife, Ian Cairns had been demonstrably more perceptive of signs of an affair between Beth Barnard and his brother-in-law, Fergus.

'In January this year, I did mention to my wife that I had noticed Beth and Fergus just looking at one another over the stockyard fence and I had felt that there was some feeling which had concerned me,' he explained.

'There was another incident in March whilst Fergus and

Vivienne were at our house which involved a picture from the Penguin Parade Christmas party involving members of our family and Beth. One particular picture was of Beth and Fergus sitting together along with other members of the family and when it was shown to Vivienne, I noticed she obviously took offence to it.'

Ian's perception of the developing romance between Beth and Fergus was, as it eventuated, very accurate.

Ian took his narrative to the night of Monday 22 September: '... at approximately 10.10pm, my wife [Marnie] received a brief phone call from Vivienne saying, "Fergus needs some stitches – please come and look after the children".'

Ian told O'Connor that Marnie had gone directly to Vivienne and Fergus's house, and after he had 'squared away the kitchen' he too joined her there. Ian described the Cameron home thus: 'There were a number of signs of a struggle which included the heater in the family room being tipped up, drops of blood on the kitchen bench, broken glass near the auto tray in the dining room, papers in the study in disarray and further evidence of blood. I also noticed that there was a singlet and shirt covered in blood in a corner in the bathroom.

'The two children were asleep in their bedroom.'

Cairns told O'Connor that he stayed for about an hour and a half before returning home at 11.15pm. Cairns recalled that when Marnie returned home she told him Fergus would stay the night at their house and that all three of them [Vivienne, Marnie and Fergus] had had a 'calm and objective talk'. Ian said that, after hearing that everything was all right, he went to bed.

Ian Cairns continued his account with the events of the morning of Tuesday 23 September.

'I was up the next morning at approximately 7am. I checked on Fergus and found him to be heavily asleep. I attended to some farm duties and gave [Marnie] a cup of tea at 7.20am. I continued on with other duties and took a phone call from my sister-in-law Pamela at approximately 7.45 or 7.50. She asked, "What's going on?" and I told her that Fergus and Vivienne had had a difference of opinion last night and that Fergus was at my place and Vivienne at home with the children. I then told her that I would talk to her when I saw her and left the phone,' Cairns told O'Connor.

'I then proceeded to Fergus's shearing shed in my car to collect the Toyota Land Cruiser tray for the hay feed out. When I arrived, the Land Cruiser wasn't there and I presumed Vivienne had used it to take their eldest child to the school bus which comes about 8.10am.

'Marnie had told me previously that Vivienne was travelling to Melbourne that morning to stay with her brother... I wondered if anything was wrong with her own car as it was not normal practice to take the Land Cruiser. I went to their Holden which was parked in the garage and turned the ignition key. I noticed that the petrol gauge was on empty and decided to fill it with petrol and service the car in preparation for her trip to Melbourne. The farm has its own petrol tank. I then returned to my house to see if anything was wrong.'

Ian Cairns told Detective O'Connor that after he returned to his farmhouse, he had received a telephone call from Pamela and Donald Cameron who told him that both Vivienne and the Land Cruiser were missing. Donald had said he would come over to Ian's house.

When Donald arrived, he and Ian spoke to Fergus who urged them to go to Beth's house and tell her about the previous night's argument. According to Ian, Fergus said, 'I am concerned for Beth'.

Ian described what happened next: 'Donald and I then proceeded to Rhyll in the Toyota Hilux ute. I feared the worst had happened and suggested to Donald that we should go to the police first, however we proceeded straight to Beth's house.

'We arrived at Beth's at approximately 9.10am and drove down the drive and parked in the backyard. We observed that Beth's Toyota ute was in a shed on our right and her white car in a carport on our left, and we believed Beth was at home.

'Donald proceeded from the car to the back door whilst I waited nearby. He opened the flywire door and knocked on the back door which opened as he did so. He then called out, "Anyone there?" or something like that and getting no response, he took a couple of paces inside. I then heard him say something like, "Oh God, the worst has happened, you'd better look."

'I then entered the back door and Donald indicated the first room on the left. I looked down and saw Beth, apparently in a sleeping bag, and she appeared to be dead. I glanced quickly around the room and it showed signs of a struggle, in particular blood on the bed and blood on the wall.

'Donald and I left the house and drove to Cowes Police Station where we spoke to Sergeant Ashe...and reported what we had seen.'

When O'Connor asked him for his impressions of Vivienne, Ian Cairns volunteered, 'I have known Vivienne for approximately nine years and always found her to be a quiet and organised person. I had not seen her display any physical violence in my presence.'

Ian Cairns signed his statement within five minutes of his wife, at 4.25pm.

Chapter Sixteen

The Hospital Visit Checks Out

INVESTIGATING OFFICERS ASSIGNED TO THE BARNARD MURDER CASE HAD HEARD FROM NUMEROUS WITNESSES THAT VIVIENNE AND FERGUS CAMERON HAD ATTENDED THE WARLEY HOSPITAL IN COWES ON THE NIGHT OF MONDAY 22 SEPTEMBER.

Nonetheless, the investigation would be incomplete unless they checked this with the staff who were on duty that night. They were, apart from members of the Cameron family, the last witnesses to see Vivienne Cameron.

Detective Senior Constable Garry Hunter was in charge of conducting interviews with Dr Allan Powles, and nursing sisters Lisa Price and Susan Bishop. On Sunday 28 September, Hunter interviewed Lisa Price at the Warley Hospital.

Lisa Price explained to the detective that she had been rostered on an afternoon shift from 2.30-11pm that Monday night.

'At about 10.15pm, Vivienne and Fergus Cameron attended at the hospital. I noticed that Fergus had a badly cut left ear and that his jumper was badly bloodstained on the back. I asked what had caused the injury to his back and Fergus told me that it was glass. Fergus appeared quite upset and was crying on and off. Vivienne was very quiet and there was nothing much said.'

Price had telephoned Dr Allan Powles who arrived shortly afterwards to attend to Fergus's injuries.

'I then assisted Dr Powles until about 10.45pm when Sue Bishop, who was the night duty sister, arrived. Sue then took over assisting Dr Powles and I left and went home. This would have been about 11.20pm.'

Asked about the Camerons and any conversation they may have had in her presence at the hospital, Lisa Price replied: 'There was no conversation between Vivienne and Fergus while I was there, but it was obvious there must have been some domestic dispute.'

Lisa Price signed her statement at 10.30am.

The detectives found Dr Allan Powles at the Island Medical Centre in the early afternoon, and his statement corresponded closely with that of Lisa Price.

'On Monday 22 September, 1986, I was on call in the evening. At about 10.20pm I received a call to attend at the Warley Hospital to treat Fergus Cameron,' he said. 'I attended at the hospital a few minutes later, approximately 10.30pm, and saw Fergus and Vivienne Cameron. I then attended to Fergus who said that he had had an accident with some glass. I noted that he had a lacerated left ear and three cuts to the back. All the injuries were cleaned and sutured. Vivienne was in the room while I attended to Fergus except for a short period when she left to make a phone call to Marnie Cairns.'

Hunter also asked Dr Powles whether he had heard any conversation between Vivienne and Fergus. Powles recalled that, while he was stitching Fergus's injuries he had asked him whether it hurt. Fergus had replied no, but Vivienne had said something like: 'Well you're luckier than I am.'

While he couldn't remember all of their conversation, Powles could recall Vivienne saying something like: 'I'm better inside, but no good with this shit.' According to Powles, Vivienne had also suggested that Fergus stay in hospital overnight, but Powles had not considered this necessary.

Asked about Vivienne's demeanour, Powles replied: 'While I was treating Fergus, I noticed that Vivienne seemed upset and tense.'

Powles had left the hospital at around 11.45pm, leaving nurse Susan Bishop to finish cleaning Fergus Cameron's ear.

The next day, Monday 29 September, Susan Bishop came to the Cowes Police Station to give her account of the night of Monday 22 September, 1986.

Nurse Bishop explained the events to Garry Hunter: 'When I arrived at work on this night, I noticed a Holden sedan, khaki green colour, parked out the front at a funny angle to the kerb. I then went inside and met Lisa Price and started handover from her.

'She advised that Fergus and Vivienne Cameron were at the hospital and that Fergus was badly cut and they would not say how it had happened. We then discussed their reasons for confidentiality and didn't take the matter any further at this stage.

'We then went to check on the dangerous drugs and this was the first time I saw Fergus and Vivienne. Fergus was lying on the table being attended to by Dr Powles and Vivienne was standing next to the table. I know Fergus and Vivienne and they were obviously embarrassed. I acknowledged their presence and then assisted Dr Powles with some sterile equipment.

'At some time Vivienne asked to use the telephone and Lisa took her away to use it. Lisa then left the hospital and went home and I checked on the other patients. I then remained in the office until Dr Powles came out and asked if there was a male bed available. I informed him that there was and he then went back to Vivienne and Fergus. There was some discussion about whether Fergus should stay in hospital or go home. Vivienne wanted him to stay in hospital but the doctor didn't think it was necessary.

'It was then decided that Fergus would go home and I assisted Dr Powles with bandaging Fergus and dressing the wounds. Dr Powles then left and I completed the task.

'Fergus then got dressed with Vivienne's assistance and they left the hospital. I saw them to the door and then locked the door after them. This would have been between 12 and 12.30am, but no later... I didn't see Vivienne or Fergus again that night.'

Hunter asked Susan Bishop what Vivienne had been wearing at the time. Nurse Bishop replied: 'Vivienne was wearing a pink mohair jumper with a round neck. She may have had a skivvy or something underneath because I remember something around her neck, blue faded jeans and black ankle boots and a scarf around her hair.'

Asked if Vivienne had any blood on her, Susan Bishop replied: 'I did not notice any blood on her or her clothing.'

Chapter Seventeen
Michael

It was detective Jack McFayden's job to interview Michael Latham, a young man who became a close friend and confidante of Beth in the final months of her life.

McFayden chose to speak with Latham at his sports shop in Cowes on Monday 29 September, 1986.

It soon became obvious to the detective that, judging from the young man's response to his questions, Michael had been very fond of Beth. Michael told McFayden that he had first met Beth at the Penguin Parade about a year earlier when he had started working there on a part-time basis. He told the detective that he, like everybody else who had known her, had called her Beth, rather than Elizabeth. 'She seemed to get on well with everyone', he said.

Michael explained how their friendship had begun: 'About two weeks after I started work at the Penguin Parade, I formed a friendship with Beth and over the last six months, we would be together almost every weekend as well as seeing each other almost every week day working at the Penguin Parade.'

It was bitterly ironic that Michael had offered to help with the lamb marking at Fergus Cameron's farm so that he could spend more time with Beth. He explained to McFayden: 'I would have been there helping for about six days and the main reason I was there was to be with Beth – as well as liking the work.'

He added: 'Since knowing Beth, I have been to her place in McFees Road in Rhyll many times and I believe we developed a very special relationship.'

When McFayden asked Michael to elaborate about the relationship, Michael seemed compelled to be specific: 'When I say we developed a special relationship, we never went to bed together or had sexual intercourse, and I didn't press this point as she said that she didn't want to have sex until she was married and she was so definite about this.'

McFayden asked Michael what he knew about Beth's relationship with Fergus Cameron. Michael replied, 'About a month ago, Beth and I were in my car when she said to me that she wanted to tell me something. She said that there was a little bit more between her and Fergus Cameron than being just good friends and she wanted me to know because I was so honest, and she was feeling dishonest in not letting me know.

'This matter wasn't discussed again until last Friday night when we were at the Isle of Wight Hotel in Cowes. We were just standing talking and she said she wanted to have a talk and told me that she was still worried about her relationship with Fergus, and me knowing about it, and she told me she decided to take three weeks off work from the Penguin Parade and Cameron's.'

According to Michael, Beth brought the same matter up again

on the following night when they, along with Beth's friend Margaret, went out for dinner to a local hotel. Michael told McFayden that Beth had said to him: 'Have you thought anything more about what we were discussing about Fergus?' Michael told Beth that he hadn't.

'I didn't say anything else as I knew it was pointless, about what was happening between her and Fergus, and she was sick anyway and I didn't want to take the matter any further.' Michael's reference to Beth being 'sick' was in the physical sense – it would later be known that she had gone to see Dr Paul Flood two days before her murder about her cold. McFayden pursued the question of Beth's relationship with Fergus Cameron and Michael seemed willing to give his personal thoughts about the affair: 'Although she never said, I assumed that the relationship between Beth and Fergus Cameron was one not of a sexual nature because of what she told me of her beliefs of sex before marriage – strongly disapproving.'

Michael may have chosen to ignore the signs, but McFayden knew differently – having interviewed Fergus Cameron the previous Thursday. Fergus had freely admitted the sexual nature of his relationship with Beth.

Michael told McFayden about the last time he had seen Beth alive. 'Last Sunday morning at about 11am, on 21 September 1986, was the last time I saw Beth alive. She came into my sports shop in Cowes and appeared to be in good spirits, and said she was looking forward to Tuesday night as we were going out somewhere in Melbourne to a band. When I say we, I mean Beth and her brother Doug and another girlfriend Jackie, who I think comes from Adelaide but I don't know her other name, and myself.

'Beth was in the shop for about 15 to 20 minutes and left.'

Michael told McFayden that he had spoken to Beth that Sunday afternoon and he had said to her that the break from work would be good for her. '...and that was the last contact I had with her.'

On 25 September, the following death notice appeared in *The Sun* newspaper:

BARNARD *Beth: My life has been enriched by your love and kindness which you shared with everyone. Friendships like ours come once in a lifetime. Thank you for being part of mine. The memories we have will keep us strong until we meet again. You will always have a place in my heart. – Michael L*

Chapter Eighteen
The Loss of a Friend

ONE CAN ONLY IMAGINE HOW BETH'S FRIEND MARGARET FELT WHEN DETECTIVE SENIOR CONSTABLE GRAHAME INCH INTERVIEWED HER AT THE PHILLIP ISLAND PENGUIN PARADE ON TUESDAY 30 SEPTEMBER – A WEEK AFTER BETH HAD BEEN MURDERED.

He had come to her work to speak with her about her best friend and, while Inch was sensitive to her devastation at the loss of a friend, he also knew that her information could be invaluable.

Margaret told Detective Inch her full name, address and stated her occupation as the administration officer at the Penguin Parade.

Inch asked Margaret about the length of her friendship with Beth Barnard and she explained that they had met about two years earlier, when Beth had started working part-time at the Penguin Parade. They had, she told the detective, formed a very close friendship.

Inch asked Margaret about Beth's relationship with Fergus Cameron. Margaret said she had been fully aware of the relationship and, indeed, had spent considerable time discussing the affair with Beth.

'...approximately 12 months after Beth had been working at the Penguin Parade, I noticed that she had formed a close relationship with another parade ranger, Fergus Cameron. This was apparent as when they were at work, they would always be together and the way that they would look at one another gave me the opinion that they had a special relationship.'

Margaret told Inch that since meeting Beth, their friendship had grown stronger and that their friendship had developed further during a month long trip to the Maldive Islands that she had taken with Beth and Deborah. 'After that trip,' she said, 'Beth started to confide in me in more personal matters, although she never spoke to me about any relationship with Fergus other than that they were really good friends and shared the same interests.'

During the interview Margaret began talking to Inch about Michael Latham whom, she said, had started work at the Penguin Parade around Christmas 1985. Margaret knew Michael before he began working at the Parade, because she had worked for him at his sporting goods store in Cowes.

Margaret explained: 'After he [Michael] had been working at the Parade for a couple of months, I was having a conversation with him about a couple of young girls that worked at the parade having a bit of a crush on him. When I told him this, he said that he was not really interested, but thought Beth was really great.'

Margaret said Michael's interest in Beth didn't really surprise her because there were many young men on the Island who were attracted to Beth.

Margaret told Inch about the admirer who would leave flowers at Beth's house when she told the detective: '...at times she would have a house full of flowers from admirers. Beth was a very popular girl with all people, as she had a bright and kind personality along with good looks.'

Margaret also explained that during the previous eight months a group of young people including Beth, Margaret, Margaret's boyfriend Robert, and Michael would meet often for dinner at various places on the Island or in nearby towns. 'The group,' she explained to Inch, 'would not always be the same, but Michael always seemed to be there with Beth and it was obvious that he was taken with her.'

According to Margaret, Beth often spoke about Michael – usually saying that he was a good, kind friend, but that she wasn't interested in him in the same way he was interested in her. 'Beth thought that Michael was infatuated with her and couldn't really be in love with her as she was just so different to him.'

Asked when she realised the serious nature of the relationship between Beth and Fergus Cameron, Margaret replied: 'Approximately two months ago, I went over to Beth's one Friday night and Fergus was there also. This was the first time that I had seen the two of them together other than in the work environment. The two appeared to be in love with each other as they were sitting together and holding hands and cuddling.

'After this night, Beth became closer to me and confided in me more about her relationship with Fergus. She used to say things like it was really difficult, because they couldn't be together and that his little boys were really important to him and that she wouldn't be able to have a normal relationship for a while. Although Beth never spelt it out, I knew she was having a sexual relationship with Fergus by different things she'd say to me, and while we were overseas, she started to take the pill.'

Inch questioned Margaret further about Fergus, Beth and Michael.

'After that night, I saw Beth and Fergus together several times at Beth's place in McFees Road, Rhyll and one night my boyfriend, Robert and I had dinner with them. They appeared to be very happy together. Beth told me that she wanted to tell Michael about her relationship with Fergus, as she wanted to be honest with him, and didn't want him hurt as he was a friend.

'On Friday night, 19 September, 1986, I rang Beth up at home and spoke to her and asked her if she had told Michael about her relationship with Fergus yet. She said she hadn't, but intended going down to the Isle of Wight Hotel that night to see Michael and tell him about it.'

Curiously, Michael had himself told Detective Jack McFayden that Beth had told him about her relationship with Fergus a month before she died – not a mere four days as Margaret suggests.

According to Margaret, the next day, Saturday 20 September, Michael and Beth called over to Margaret's house and they had all gone to dinner at a local hotel. Margaret told Inch that while Michael had gone to the bar to order some drinks, she took the opportunity to ask Beth if she had told Michael about Fergus.

'...Beth told me that she had told Michael all about Fergus but she said that she didn't think he really heard what she was saying, and she said she didn't get any sort of reaction or reply from him.

'Beth told me that she was going to bring it up again on their trip home and ask him if he had understood what she had told him the night before.' The conversation, according to Margaret, had ceased as Michael returned with the drinks.

Margaret said she hadn't seen Beth again until Monday 22 September – Beth's last day alive. Beth had been to a travel agent to pick up some pamphlets about Darwin and spoke to Margaret about a holiday she was planning to take with her mother. '...she was really excited about it,' said Margaret.

Margaret spoke about the last time she had seen her best friend: 'She discussed both Fergus and Michael and said how it would be good to have a break from the Island, but would really miss being away from Fergus. She said that she had told Michael again about her and Fergus, but he didn't say anything, only that he had heard what she said the night before.

'Beth left my place at about 3.45pm that afternoon saying that she would ring me later in the week. She said that she was going up to Melbourne to stay with her family and meet a girlfriend, Jackie and go to the Show with her. She also said that she had invited Michael to go, as her brother Doug would be there, and that they got on well together.'

Inch finished the interview by asking Margaret whether that was the last time she had seen or heard from her friend.

Margaret's reply formed the final sentence in her four page statement: 'I haven't seen or heard from Beth since.'

Chapter Nineteen

The Scarlet Letter

'Thus she will be a living sermon against sin, until the ignominious letter be engraved upon her tombstone. It irks me, nevertheless, that the partner of her iniquity should not, at least, stand on the scaffold by her side. But he will be known! – he will be known! – he will be known!'

From *The Scarlet Letter* by Nathaniel Hawthorne (1850)

NOBODY CAN SAY EXACTLY WHEN THE INVESTIGATION INTO THE KILLING OF BETH BARNARD BEGAN FOCUSSING ON THE POSSIBLE SIGNIFICANCE OF AN OBSCURE WORK OF NINETEENTH CENTURY AMERICAN FICTION, *THE SCARLET LETTER* BY NATHANIEL HAWTHORNE.

In the days after Beth's murder, stories quickly spread through the small community on Phillip Island that a large symbol had been carved into her body. Initially, the talk circulating among local farmers, shopkeepers and reporters was that the symbol was a 'V' – ostensibly most people thought this made sense because the letter could have stood for 'Vivienne'.

However, for the detectives investigating the murder and the pathologist who performed the post-mortem examination, there could be no mistaking that the letter carved deeply into Beth's chest and abdomen was an 'A'.

On 24 September, 1986, pathologist Dr Anderson noted in his autopsy report that Beth's lower chest had 'a series of slashes which formed an 'A' shape, with the point of the 'A' directed toward the head'. He went on to meticulously describe and document each slash and its length and depth.

It was three days after Beth's body was discovered that news of the 'A' was disclosed in Melbourne's *Sun News Pictorial*. Two days later, on Sunday 28 September, Melbourne's now defunct *Sunday Press* newspaper published a more detailed article on Beth's murder and Vivienne's disappearance. Under the headline *Who Killed Quiet, Sweet, Beth?* the *Sunday Press* said the letter 'A' carved into Beth's body added a 'macabre twist' to the killing. The journalist wrote that Phillip Island residents spoke to him about 'the rumours and theories which have flowed thick and fast since the night Beth Barnard died'.

Les Hams, a reporter on the *Phillip Island Sun* – a local newspaper that has since closed – was quoted [incorrectly] as saying he had 'heard five different ones [rumours] between getting out of my car and the office door'.

While the *Sunday Press* alluded to the rumours surrounding the murder – and particularly the 'A' – it failed to articulate them.

Much of the talk focussed on the possible involvement of the occult. This was perhaps a natural reaction for many on Phillip Island – when an attractive, young local woman is brutally murdered and a respected mother of two vanishes – both on the same night, it was easy for some on the Island to blame someone as vague as a devil worshipper. In Satanic symbolism, the letter A represents anarchy and the denial of authority. It can also be a symbol for the Antichrist. If a Satanist was responsible for the death and disappearance of the two women, it would have been a devil they could fight – a person whom they could capture and imprison. However, when information began to slowly filter through the media, that Vivienne Cameron was a chief suspect, the rumours of devil worshippers and anarchy soon abated. The town had to come to terms with the fact that one of their own had 'snapped'. Many would forever find this almost too painful to accept.

Like many police officers, Detective Rory O'Connor never had an academic interest in seventeenth century American literature. However, in the days after Beth's body was discovered he began looking at a possible connection between Nathaniel Hawthorne's *The Scarlet Letter* and Beth's murder, after being told by Vivienne's sister that Vivienne had read the Hawthorne's Gothic romance about a 'fallen woman'. Set in the puritanical environment of seventeenth century Boston, *The Scarlet Letter* traces the plight of Hester Prynne, a young woman who attracted the wrath of the Calvinist community in which she lived by conceiving a child. Hester Prynne was in fact married, but her husband had yet to arrive in the country, and therefore, the child was that of another man. Hawthorne wrote of Hester Prynne's persecution after giving birth to her daughter called Pearl. After going before the judges it was deemed that Hester should wear forever the scarlet letter 'A' on her clothing, to proclaim to her community that she was an adulteress. '*...she would become the general symbol at which the preacher and moralist might point, and in which they might vivify and embody their images of women's frailty and sinful passion. Thus the young and* *pure would be taught to look at her, with the scarlet letter flaming on her breast ... as the figure, the body, the reality of sin.'*

Throughout the story, Hester Prynne never reveals the father of her child, but a young clergyman, Arthur Dimmesdale, eventually becomes consumed by grief and in a final, dramatic scene, he admits publicly that he is the father of Prynne's daughter. Dimmesdale rips open his shirt – to reveal a self-inflicted scar on his chest – his own scarlet letter. Dimmesdale then dies.

O'Connor could see the relevance of *The Scarlet Letter* if, indeed, Vivienne Cameron had read it. In death, Beth Barnard had been branded with 'the scarlet letter'. Like Hester Prynne, Beth Barnard was an 'adulteress' – if not in the literal, but certainly the literary sense – in the eyes of some people in the small Phillip Island community. Certainly in the eyes of Vivienne, 'that little bitch' [as, according to Fergus Cameron's statement, Vivienne had referred to Beth] was breaking up her marriage.

Had Vivienne killed the object of her husband's affection and then recalled to mind Hawthorn's *The Scarlet Letter*, in order to inflict the dead woman with the huge 'A' symbol?

However, a stumbling block in this theory remains the question of whether Vivienne would have had sufficient composure, after mutilating Beth, in what is still regarded as a crime of passion, to carefully carve such a symbol into her chest and abdomen. O'Connor had little doubt that if Vivienne had carefully planned the crime that she would almost certainly have been responsible for the 'A'. Certainly if Vivienne had suicided by jumping from the Phillip Island bridge – consistent with a later coronial finding – she would have had few qualms about carving a symbol into the body of her victim which would indicate her guilt. However, because Vivienne's body was never found and in light of the alleged phone conversation between Vivienne and a friend after she was assumed to have killed herself, it would make little sense for her to leave such evidence of her guilt on the body.

Detective O'Connor was aware that if, indeed, Vivienne had carefully planned Beth's murder and mutilation, and her subsequent suicide, there was little supporting evidence. She had made no attempt to finalise her affairs or to justify her actions with a suicide note.

The day before her disappearance she had worked, as usual, at the Phillip Island Community House where one of her colleagues said she had 'been acting normally'.

The colleague recalled an interesting conversation with her friend Vivienne the week before her disappearance.

'You always look so calm and contented,' the colleague had said to Vivienne while the two had made the short trip by car to San Remo for a meeting. To her surprise, Vivienne had replied, 'I'm not happy. I'd like to have the boys educated away from the Island. Farm life is not a comfortable life – sometimes I wish I could just take the boys and leave. My life is for the boys.'

Vivienne told her work friend that she was planning to leave Fergus and take her two boys to live in Melbourne. This was not news to the friend, who had heard the circulating rumour of an imminent Cameron divorce.

O'Connor had also been told, by many people on the Island who knew Vivienne Cameron, of her selfless dedication to her children – how she would take them to the doctors at the least sign of a sniffle and how she devoted herself to their complete well being. He pondered whether Vivienne was the type of woman who would carefully premeditate such a brutal murder and then take her own life in the knowledge that she would never see her beloved children again.

One close friend summed up the feelings of many in the

community when she said: 'I can't believe she did it [killed Beth].
I can't see her not leaving something for the boys,' the friend said.
When asked what she meant, the friend said: 'Some kind of note
or something to say goodbye. She thought the world of those kids.'

Chapter Twenty
Women Who Kill

FEMALE MURDERERS ARE RARE IN AUSTRALIA AND WOMEN WHO KILL OTHER WOMEN ARE EVEN MORE INFREQUENT – SO MUCH SO THAT THE CORONIAL SERVICES OF VICTORIA HAVE AN AVERAGE OF ONE SUCH CASE PER YEAR.

When the Coronial Inquiry into the death of Beth Barnard was heard at the Korumburra Court on 20 August 1987, the Coroner, Mr B Maher, found that: 'The deceased was located at her residence in McFees Rd, Rhyll, with extensive injuries to her body; such injuries were caused by knife wounds and were inflicted by another person. AND I FURTHER FIND that VIVIENNE CAMERON contributed to the cause of death.'

Under the *Coroners Act 1985 (Victoria)*, it is the coroner's duty to investigate all aspects of a death explicitly, excluding issues of direct criminal liability. Section 19, part 3 of the act states: 'A coroner must not include in a finding or comment, any statement that a person is or may be guilty of an offence'. However, section 19, part 1(e) of the act also states that the coroner investigating a death must find, if possible, 'the identity of any person who contributed to the cause of death'.

It is clear the coroner, Mr Maher, considered that Vivienne Cameron was involved in the death of Beth Barnard, but in accordance with the Coroners Act under which he operated, he stopped short of saying that Vivienne was Beth's killer.

However, the Coronial finding that Vivienne Cameron did contribute to the cause of death in the Barnard killing, was the only case in Victoria in 1986, with a female murderer and a female victim.

In *Violence in Australia* (1991) – published by the Institute of Criminology in Canberra – Kenneth Polk and David Ranson refer in their chapter, 'Homicide in Victoria', to the Cameron– Barnard case. In their exploration of the relationships between killers and their victims, Polk and Ranson examine Vivienne's involvement in Beth's murder in what they refer to as a 'rare twist' in the area of homicide – women who have killed other women. Of the Cameron–Barnard case, they concluded: 'This is the only case in these files of jealous rage of a woman directed at the rival for her sexual partner's affections.'

Polk and Ranson cite research which shows that only 15–20 per cent of murderers are women, and that most women who kill do so to rid themselves of a violent male partner. Victorian Coronial Services recorded that in four out of the six cases in the period of 1985–86 where women killed their male partners, they did so as a defence against violence towards them or their children. In the same period, Coronial Services records show that 27 men killed their female partners as opposed to the six women who killed their male partners.

While recorded cases of female killers in Victoria are small in number, they offer a curious contrast to the prevalence of similar cases in the United States where, according to Polk and Ranson, 'often the number of women who kill their husbands is equal to, or perhaps even greater than, the number of husbands who kill their wives'. It is obvious that overseas patterns do not always extend to Australian shores.

Polk and Ranson examine the methods Australian women employ to rid themselves of violent male partners. 'A striking feature of the most straightforward of these killings is the single nature of the fatal wound, a feature distinguishing these cases pathologically from the multiple injuries observed in the male offender...'

In her book *Homicide: The Social Reality* (1986), Alison Wallace concludes that the majority of homicides involving male offenders and female victims could be viewed as an expression 'of their power and control over their wives'. She wrote that either separation or jealousy were the main causes of such murders – the deadly principle: 'if I can't have you, then no one can'.

'Women who killed their husbands against a backdrop of violence killed in response to and because of violence perpetrated by their husbands on them and/or other members of their family,' says Wallace.

According to Dr Patricia Easteal of the Canberra-based Australian Institute of Criminology, men are responsible for 75 per cent of domestic murders in Australia. The small number of women who killed their partners in Australia had almost always been battered to the point where the murder was an act of self defence, she said. Comparably, most men who killed their spouses or former spouses had a history of domestic violence, Dr Easteal said.

An exploration of homicide patterns in Victoria and the wider

Australian community offers some insight into the Cameron–Barnard murder – both where it fits and diverges from commonly observed patterns. Polk and Ranson found: 'Homicide in New South Wales is a crime which typically occurs between intimates; four out of five victims knew their attacker, and in a majority of cases, their relationship was a close one. The family was the most common venue for these homicides.'

Polk and Ranson quote research as showing 'that homicide occurs about half the time in a home of either the victim or the offender, that it is slightly more likely to take place on a Saturday in contrast to other days of the week, and that the great majority of homicides take place between 3pm and 3am. Guns are, slightly, the most frequent weapon [used in roughly one-third of the cases], followed by knives...'

Beth Barnard was murdered in the early hours of a Tuesday morning rather than a Saturday night, and the time of death was never established, but she was killed by one of the most common methods – stabbing. Beth also died in her own home. However, the most unique aspect of Beth's murder lies in the Coronial finding that Vivienne Cameron 'contributed to the cause of death'.

If indeed, Vivienne Cameron did kill Beth Barnard – and many accept this unequivocally – then she is atypical of Australian murderers, most of whom are male [80–85 per cent], over 25 years old [66 per cent], and have previous criminal records [55 per cent].

Assuming that Vivienne did kill Beth, perhaps the most profound difference between Vivienne Cameron and other Australian domestic murderers is that the offender is more likely to kill their partner rather than the object of their partner's affections. While, according to Fergus Cameron's police statement, Vivienne viciously attacked her husband with a wineglass during a jealous rage – only hours before Beth was killed – it would seem that the true object of her wrath was not her husband, but his lover.

If the unequivocal belief that Vivienne Cameron murdered Beth Barnard is proved, then she has a male counterpart in another unrelated crime in the same year – 1986. Contained in Coronial files is the case of a husband who killed his estranged wife's lover. The husband had told a friend that the new man in his wife's life 'was a con man', and would be 'fixed up'. The husband went to the man's house and fatally shot him. He then wrote notes confessing to the crime saying that the man had ruined all their lives. The husband's car was later found abandoned on the Great Ocean Road and he was never seen or heard from again. Although Vivienne left no notes of confession, the two cases bear a similarity – especially in light of the fact that both vehicles were found near water and the bodies of both Vivienne and the husband in the above case were never found.

To put the Cameron–Barnard case in perspective of the female offender/female victim category, it is worth exploring two other cases where a woman has murdered another woman – one case in 1987 and another case in 1988.

In the 1987 case, two women – Kim aged 29 and Sue aged 26, both having served sentences together in Fairlea Women's Prison, began an argument involving the affections of a male prisoner that they had both been writing to. According to a case synopsis on file at the Melbourne Coroner's Court, Kim had taken heroin twice, as well as 'some tablets', on the day she was killed by Sue. Sue had taken two Serapax and two Valium tablets. The two women began arguing and, according to a witness, after the two women had come to blows, Sue 'stormed into the kitchen and obtained a knife. She yelled, "You reckon I'm a cunt, do you?" and stabbed Kim.' Sue was charged and convicted with manslaughter – sentenced to five years prison, with a minimum of four years.

The second case, occurring in 1988, involved Cheryl aged 31 and Deborah aged 21. The women lived in the same block of council flats – Cheryl with her six-month-old baby and Deborah with her lesbian partner, Tina. Deborah had a history of chronic drug abuse and an extensive criminal history, including many convictions for theft and being found in the possession of drugs of dependence.

Cheryl and her baby passed Deborah and Tina in the street and became involved in an argument. It is thought the two women held Cheryl responsible for some local graffiti which read, 'Tina is a lesi bitch'. During the argument, Deborah punched Cheryl, grabbed her by the hair and threw her to the ground. Cheryl managed to get herself and her young baby away.

Angered by the attack, Cheryl armed herself with a wooden baton and sought help from two male friends whom she told, '[I'm going to] go down and get them two bitches'. Cheryl, once outside the residence of Deborah and Tina, called to them, 'Now come out and fight me, I haven't got my baby with me now...' Deborah obliged and brought a knife with her. Cheryl, seeing the knife, ran to her car only to be pursued and stabbed by Deborah. The knife pierced Cheryl's right pulmonary artery and she died shortly afterwards.

The assistant police surgeon later stated that Deborah had 'features of an anti-social personality disorder'. She was found guilty of manslaughter and sentenced to three years in prison – with a minimum of 18 months.

The facts surrounding the Cameron-Barnard case bear little resemblance to the above two cases where the offenders both had criminal records, and histories of drug abuse.

Australia has been relatively insulated from the crime trends seen in other countries. History has given Australia few notorious female criminals compared to countries such as England and America. Infamous male killers are universally known and remembered. Names such as those of Melbourne's Hoddle and Queen Street killers – Julian Knight and Frank Vitkovic – as well as infamous killers from overseas like Charles Manson, Ted Bundy, David Berkowitz [Son of Sam], Albert DeSalvo [The Boston Strangler], Jack the Ripper, and Dr Crippen, still send shivers up the collective spines of law-abiding citizens and police forces. Indeed, infamous females are only slightly less fearsome. England's Myra Hindley, responsible, with her lover, Ian Brady, for the 'Moors Murders' in which children were brutally killed and buried on the moors, and American nurse Genene Jones, who killed 13 children in her care, at the hospital in which she worked, are shocking examples of the potential for females to commit brutal crimes.

Fortunately, Australia has barely been touched by such extreme cases of female violence. Dr Paul Wilson, in his book *A Life of Crime*, writes, 'I firmly believe that the amounts and kinds of violence that occur in a society tell us much about the values of that society.' Australian trends have yet to follow overseas patterns in many forms of murder. The phenomenon that Professor Geoffrey Blainey labelled the 'tyranny of distance' may, in fact, serve as a buffer zone against patterns emerging from overseas, such as the advent of the serial killer and violent drug-gang warfare as portrayed in the American movie *Colors*.

Australian history gives few examples of women killers. In 1894, a Melbourne woman, Frances Knorr, was hanged for the murder of three babies. The 25-year-old Mrs Knorr had been paid to mind the babies on a full-time basis by their unwed mothers. This 'baby minding' was a common practice in this era, as it was frowned upon for an unmarried woman to have a child. Mrs Knorr found it easier to accept the fee and the monthly payments from the mothers, while their babies lay buried in the garden of her rented Brunswick home. The next tenant was also interested in gardens – although for not the same reasons as Mrs Knorr – and it didn't take him long to make the gruesome discovery. Mrs Knorr was convicted and hanged for her crimes.

The last woman to hang in Australia, Jean Lee, went to the gallows in 1951 in Melbourne's Pentridge Gaol. Jean Lee had entered the world of prostitution during the Second World War – catering to the scores of [mainly American] soldiers crowding into Australia's capital cities at the time. She had a lengthy criminal record and Jean Lee eventually sought the services of a pimp. Together they developed a plan: Jean would lure a victim into a compromising situation, and her pimp would arrive home 'unexpectedly', playing the part of an outraged husband. The situation would invariably be resolved by the victim paying 'compensation' to the husband. It was only a matter of time before a prospective client refused Jean's enticements. She cured his reluctance by smashing a bottle over his head and repeatedly bashing the old man unconscious with a piece of wood. He died from his brutal injuries. Jean Lee died on the gallows.

More recently, Australians were shocked by the so-called 'Vampire Killing' in 1989, by a Queensland woman, Tracey Wigginton. Wigginton, aged 24, was a lesbian and interested in devil worship and the occult. She also drank animal blood. Tracey Wigginton had such a forceful personality that she convinced a number of friends to assist her to kill someone and drink the blood of their random victim. 'I can't have solid food,' she is alleged to have said, 'I need blood to survive on.'

The bloodied body of Edward Baldock – a blameless family man – was found near the South Brisbane Sailing Club with multiple stab wounds. Later Wigginton described the killing to the police: '...I stabbed him... I withdrew the knife and I stabbed him on the side of the neck. I stabbed him on the other side of his neck and I continuously stabbed him. I then grabbed him by the hair... and pulled him back, stabbing him in the front of the throat and at that stage he was still alive... I stabbed him in the back of the neck again, trying to get into the bones, I presume, and cut the nerves. I than sat in front of the tilt-a-doors and watched him die.' Wigginton later told her friends that she had drunk the blood of her victim.

While Vivienne Cameron's disappearance and presumed death, and not least, the murder of Beth Barnard, dealt a shocking blow to the Phillip Island community and most notably to the families and friends of both women, the case can be viewed more analytically as one of the greatest, albeit least publicised, domestic tragedies in recent Australian criminal history.

If the Coroner's finding that Vivienne contributed to Beth's death is accepted, then this is a story of an admired and respected housewife, a loving mother and dedicated wife, being driven to uncharacteristic violence by her jealousy towards an unfaithful husband and his younger, more outgoing and sexually attractive lover.

However, the fact remains that Vivienne Cameron cannot be considered to be a murderess in the genre of Tracey Wigginton, Frances Knorr or Jean Lee – women who had all carefully planned their killings for money or blood lust. Again, the case books and the statistics will not tell the full story of Vivienne Cameron who, it can be argued, had little to gain personally out of her alleged violence and suicide. Indeed, it can be argued that Vivienne

Cameron – through the act of murder, which the coroner found she contributed to – lost everything dear to her: her husband, her children, her reputation and – if she did jump from the bridge – her life.

Fergus Cameron was also dealt a crushing blow as a result, it can be argued, of his marital infidelity. While it is accepted that many married men are unfaithful to their wives, few, if any, in Australia have lost in such violent circumstances, both their wife and lover in one day.

While searching for motives and analysing Vivienne Cameron's departure from the stereotypes of Australian murderers, perhaps the most tragic manifestation of the violence and jealousy that apparently gripped Vivienne should not be overlooked: the loss of an innocent young woman, Beth Barnard.

Chapter Twenty-one
As It Stands

An inquest for Vivienne Cameron was held a mere 22 months after her disappearance.

On 21 July 1988, Coroner Mr Maher, the same coroner who had conducted Beth Barnard's inquest 11 months earlier, made a very specific finding:

> I, Mr B J Maher, Coroner, having investigated the death of Vivienne Janice Cameron, find that the identity of the deceased was Vivienne Janice Cameron and that the death occurred on 23rd September, 1986 near the bridge which separates Phillip Island from the mainland in the following circumstances. During the night of the 22nd and 23rd day of September, 1986 Elizabeth Barnard died from knife wounds in her chest and that Vivienne Janice Cameron has not been seen since 1.00am on the 23rd day of September, 1986. On the night in question, it is believed that Vivienne Janice Cameron was driving [a] Toyota Land Cruiser... This vehicle was

found abandoned near the said bridge on the Phillip Island side of the bridge. Despite an intensive Police search, no trace has been found of the said Vivienne Janice Cameron with whom they wished to speak concerning the death of Elizabeth Barnard. Although her body has not been found, I am satisfied that she is dead and that she leapt from the bridge into the water. And I further find that the deceased contributed to the cause of death.

Interestingly, years later, a close relative of Vivienne Cameron spoke of briefing a Queen's Counsel to appear at Vivienne's Inquest to represent her interests. The relative said that the QC and several family members made the long drive from Melbourne and arrived at the Korumburra Court House before the scheduled Inquest time of 10am – only to find that the Inquest was already over. If the relative's story is accurate, one can only wonder how the Coroner had time to consider the vast amount of evidence and come to such a specific conclusion.

In 1910, a French detective named Edmond Locard formulated what became known as the 'exchange principle'. The basis of his theory was that the criminal always leaves something at the crime scene and always takes away traces of the scene with him or her. According to the exchange principle, the criminal may leave fingerprints, footprints, blood, sweat, saliva, semen or strands of hair or clothing fibres at the scene of the crime. Similarly, he or she takes away potential evidence such as blood and hair from the victim, fibres from the victim's clothing and, perhaps on his or her shoes, soil or vegetation particular to the area where the crime was committed.

Such 'contact traces', as they are now known, form the basis for forensic detection work today. Detectives, crime scene officers and fingerprint experts look for evidence that connects suspects or the offender with the victim.

Despite all the thorough work of police like crime scene examiners Brian Gamble and Hughie Peters involved in the Barnard murder case, the only contact trace that might have linked Vivienne Cameron with the murder scene at Beth Barnard's house was a few droplets of Type A blood found on the path outside the Barnard house, a towel found in Beth's bathroom, and a face washer found in the Land Cruiser. Interestingly, Marnie Cairns speaks of a towel and a face washer that she saw when she first went to the Camerons' house to mind the children: 'I went into the toilet and noticed a pile of blood-soaked clothing consisting of a singlet, T shirt, a pale blue shirt from the Penguin Parade, a face washer and a towel. There were also some tissues in the basin which had blood on them. Ian arrived shortly after and I showed him the clothing. He suggested that we leave it where it was and not touch it.' One would assume Marnie mentioned the towel and face-washer along with other bloodstained items because they too had blood on them, but only the pink tissue and the blue shirt tested positive for Fergus's blood. The singlet is not mentioned in the list of items taken by police for examination. Nor is there a towel or a face washer mentioned as being taken from the Cameron house.

According to Dr Bentley Atchison, a scientific officer who works for the State Forensic Science Laboratory, who analysed the blood-stained items from the murder scene, Vivienne Cameron is among the 38 per cent of Victorians who have Type A blood.

Presumably if, as the Coroner determined, Vivienne contributed to Beth's murder, she must have left other traces of her presence in the Barnard residence. Apparently not. There were no fingerprints on the murder weapon found near the body even though the knife hadn't been wiped and was still heavily stained with Beth's blood. Despite such heavy staining on both the blade and the handle of the knife, Sergeant Michael Rilen from the fingerprint bureau was unable to obtain any fingerprints from the knife. Curiously, Rilen was also unable to obtain any 'identifiable' fingerprints when he examined the Land Cruiser which was found near the Phillip Island-San Remo bridge – a bridge from which, the coroner decided, despite a profound lack of supporting evidence, Vivienne had chosen to jump to end her life.

It is known that Vivienne had been wearing a pink mohair jumper on the night Beth died. However, no traces of mohair were found at Beth's house or in the Land Cruiser. Again, if we use Locard's universally accepted theory as a guide, there is no evidence that Vivienne Cameron took any 'contact traces' or evidence away from the murder scene. Even though the experts agree that whoever killed Beth would have been soaked with her blood when they left her house that night, no blood of Beth's type [O, PGM 1] was found in the Land Cruiser which, it has been assumed, Vivienne had driven to and from the murder scene.

Indeed, one of the forensic experts assigned to this case, Brian Gamble, says he was 'surprised' that no blood of Beth's type was found in the Land Cruiser. The small amount of blood that was found in the Land Cruiser was Type A blood – again, Vivienne Cameron's type and that of 38 per cent of the population.

Nonetheless, some of the investigating officers remain adamant that Vivienne Cameron jumped from the Phillip Island-San Remo Bridge even though there is little or no evidence to suggest this happened. Her body was never found during an extensive search conducted by Sergeant Geoff Frost of the search and rescue squad, who was confident that if Vivienne had jumped from the bridge there was a strong possibility of locating her body. Failing that, he believes that at the very least some other evidence – such as the gold-rimmed glasses she was wearing when she disappeared – would have been found, thus supporting the theory that she had jumped. It seems likely that her glasses would have fallen off during a 10-metre leap from the bridge, or that one of her shoes, or perhaps the floral scarf she had been wearing, would have been found during the extensive land and sea search.

The many police involved in the Barnard murder case are duty-bound to support the verdict of the coroner – a verdict which found Vivienne had 'contributed' to the murder before throwing herself from the bridge.

To this day, however, the finding that Vivienne jumped from the bridge is based largely on the premise that the Camerons' Land Cruiser was seen close to the bridge, very early on the morning of Vivienne's disappearance. However, this premise – and subsequently the suicide theory if it is based on this premise alone – would appear to be seriously flawed.

The statement of Wayne Hunt, a bakery driver who was thought to have seen the Land Cruiser that morning, muddles the suicide theory considerably. In the statement – taken by detective Garry Hunter on 27 September, 1986 – Hunt made it clear that he took little notice of whatever type of vehicle it was that had been parked near the bridge that morning.

'I cannot say what type of car it was or colour, all I can say is that there was a car parked there,' Hunt said. 'I just glanced and kept on going, but thought it was strange for it to be parked there at that time because normally there is nothing there. I thought it must have been someone using the toilet and didn't think any more about it.'

Some detectives assigned to the case would later say that Hunt had definitely seen the Land Cruiser at five that morning – information they saw as vital because, if the car was there that early it was, to them, and subsequently the coroner, a strong indication that she had jumped from the bridge.

However, that afternoon it was clearly the Camerons' Land Cruiser parked in Forrest Avenue. And it was clear that it had been found by a member of the Cameron family. Ironically the vehicle could be clearly seen from the Phillip Island end of the bridge and if it had been there since early morning the detectives, driving back and forth from Wonthaggi and Melbourne, had passed it, unnoticed, many times during the day. Pam Cameron also didn't notice it earlier when she had gone to the pottery shop, but she *had* noticed a police car parked near there. This was before she had heard about Beth's murder. Oddly, whoever was in the police car didn't notice the Land Cruiser either.

Even if Vivienne did kill herself that night, it seems unlikely she would have done so by jumping from the bridge. Not least, because there is a good chance she would have survived the fall and, because it is the only thoroughfare to the Island, there would have been a chance that a passing motorist might have seen her, or worse, tried to stop her. According to local police, nobody had ever suicided from the bridge before and those who do suicide on the Island usually choose to jump into the treacherous waters at the Nobbies, a rocky outcrop surrounded by wild surf at the south-western tip of the Island. It is also likely Vivienne would have chosen the Nobbies – like a number of disillusioned and sad people who have suicided from there – because it is close to her house in Ventnor.

Some police assigned to the case did, however, examine the possibility that Vivienne might have caught a bus after abandoning the Land Cruiser near the bridge. 'It [the Land Cruiser] was just as close to the bus stop,' one detective said. But again, this is no more credible than the suicide theory because of the uncertainty about when the vehicle found its way to the bridge.

Then of course there is the mysterious phone call from Vivienne to her friend Gillian Fraser at 10am on the day of her disappearance – some hours after it is assumed that she had jumped from the bridge. Gillian is still adamant it was Vivienne she spoke to that morning.

Gillian's friend Paula has verified that Gillian received the phone call from Vivienne at 10am on 23 September. A curious aspect of the phone call is the voices she recalls hearing in the background – voices she assumed were those of Vivienne's children. But at least one of the children was at school at the time. Was somebody with Vivienne? If so, perhaps somebody knows the truth about what happened to her and Beth.

Gillian says Vivienne's conversation that morning was hardly that of somebody who had just committed one of the most brutal murders in the Coroner's Court files. Vivienne, according to Gillian, sounded completely normal and spoke about a patchwork doll's house she wanted to buy as a gift for a friend.

A clear lack of forensic evidence near the bridge also further discounts the suicide theory. According to Detective Jack McFayden, he found no traces of blood or clothing – nothing to indicate Vivienne Cameron had jumped – when he carefully searched the bridge.

If the car Wayne Hunt saw was not the Cameron vehicle, but perhaps a traveller stopping to use the amenities at the park, it could be assumed, from Gillian Fraser's statement, that perhaps Vivienne Cameron knew nothing about the murder when she spoke to Gillian on the telephone.

Theoretically at least, it is not difficult to find reasons why Vivienne might have wanted to kill Beth. According to Fergus Cameron, Vivienne was, understandably, extremely bitter towards Beth. In his statement Fergus says that Vivienne had told him on the night of the murder: 'I'm just going to get the little bitch.' But according to Fergus's sister, Marnie Cairns, although Vivienne had earlier told her she 'could no longer feel the same way about Beth as the rest of us did,' Vivienne had also admitted, with regard to her husband's infidelity, that 'if it wasn't Beth, it probably would have been someone else'.

While there is no doubt Vivienne would have felt anger towards Beth, it is unusual – in light of research into criminal behaviour both here and overseas – that she directed her violent rage more towards 'the other woman' rather than at her own errant husband.

Of the Cameron–Barnard case the criminologists Polk and Ranson concluded: 'This is the only case in these files of jealous rage of a woman directed at the rival for her sexual partner's affections.'

In 'Violence In Australia', they cite research showing that only 15 to 20 per cent of murderers are women, and that most women who kill do so to rid themselves of a violent male partner. Victorian Coronial Services recorded that in four out of the six cases in the period of 1985–86 where women killed their male partners, they did so as a defence against violence towards them or their children. In the same period, Coronial Services records show that 27 men killed their female partners as opposed to the six women who killed their male partners.

On Monday 22 September, the day before Beth's murder and her disappearance, Vivienne confided to a work colleague she wanted to leave the Island with her two children. In light of this comment, it would have seemed that Vivienne was more likely to pack up herself and her children and leave her husband, rather than murder her husband's lover and kill herself that night. In other words, Vivienne – unlike most people who choose to murder and then kill themselves – was contemplating a future life with her children and away from her husband.

In a book by Brian Marriner, *Forensic Clues to Murder* (1991), Marriner quotes a crime writer, F Tennyson Jesse as categorising the six motives for murder: elimination, gain, revenge, jealousy, lust, and conviction. These motives, first penned in 1924, are still highly regarded as relevant today and relevant to the Barnard murder.

What was the motive behind Beth Barnard's murder? Did Vivienne's jealousy so compel her to kill her husband's lover when she believed Fergus was determined to have an affair anyway?

Was Beth's killing a 'lust' murder then? Semen was found both internally and externally in samples taken at the post-mortem examination. Because semen can only be detected for several days when it is inside the body, forensic experts say it is unusual to detect its presence externally outside the body after two days – especially with normal activities like showering and toileting. Fergus Cameron said he had sexual intercourse with Beth on Sunday 21 September, but not on the Monday night of her death. Detectives questioned many of Beth's male acquaintances, but none said they had had sex with her. DNA testing which has the capability to match hair, blood, semen and other bodily secretions to a crime suspect, had not been introduced to Australia at the time of Beth's murder in 1986. Therefore, the question of whether anyone else but Fergus Cameron had had sex with Beth on the days preceding her death remains unanswered.

In an American crime book, *Unanswered Cries* (1991), author Thomas French makes a statement that is eminently relevant to the Barnard murder case. 'One of the most terrible things about an unsolved murder is the taint of uncertainty it casts on everyone around it. If one person in our midst is capable of violently taking someone's life, then any of us may be capable – and may be scrutinised with that possibility in mind. Suddenly, the most innocent actions may be viewed in the most sinister light.'

Because Beth's killer was never brought to justice through the court system, the small community of Phillip Island is still talking, and wondering who is responsible. In a recent letter to the Phillip Island *Sentinel Times* in response to an article by journalist Richard Schmeiszl, about the imminent release of this book, a woman from an outer Melbourne suburb, wrote the following. It sums up the feelings of many people who knew the dead and missing women:

Sir, When I read Richard Schmeiszl's article about this book being written, I felt sad but very relieved. As a close friend of one of the victims involved in this tragic murder-mystery I have been waiting and wondering why the public has for so long been denied the facts and information related to this case. Too quickly this murder was dismissed – hushed up as if we, the friends and associates of the victims, should not remember or consider that these two women ever existed, or in fact that a murder had ever occurred at all. I and others do not believe that at this time, the police involved questioned a broad enough cross-section of the community, nor do we think that the investigation of the circumstances leading up to the murder – followed by a very strange disappearance of one of the victims – was sufficiently or decisively thorough or extensive. The crime still remains unsolved and there are many puzzling aspects to the case. Surely fingerprints, weapons, clothing fibres, bloodstains and identified blood groups would have some bearing as conclusive evidence as to 'who did what'. The phone call on the Tuesday morning was a reality and allegedly by one of the victims, but this was dismissed at the Coronial Inquiry. Why?

Perhaps one of the most intriguing facts is that Mrs Cameron was officially declared 'deceased' in under two years. How and why was this deemed necessary? There are many strange incidents woven throughout the saga of this murder-mystery that occurred in September, 1986 on Phillip Island.

We, the friends and associates of the victims, whoever and wherever we may be, are concerned that the local establish-ment may have the power and resources to suppress information/details of events that the ordinary citizen cannot.'

There is little doubt that the woman who wrote this letter [she did not want to be named] views Vivienne Cameron as a victim in this case. Certainly the situation that Vivienne found herself in was unenviable: a devoted wife and mother who, according to friends, worked tirelessly on the farm and at the community house, but whose life was turned upside-down by her unfaithful husband. There is little doubt she was contemplating a life for her and her children away from Fergus. And if, according to the Coronial finding, Vivienne Cameron did 'contribute to the death' of Beth Barnard, then she was a woman driven to the most extreme of crimes – by desperation and despair. If Vivienne did not kill Beth Barnard, and the available evidence against her is far from conclusive, then she and her family are themselves the victims of a grave injustice. Either way, Vivienne Cameron can, herself, be viewed as a victim.

Some police concede that the investigation into the murder and the disappearance concluded too soon. Many questions remained unanswered.

The police were hampered by a number of people on the island – with the notable exception of Fergus Cameron and his extended family – who were unwilling to speak with candour about the affairs, rumours, and deceptions preceding the murder and their personal interests in the victim.

This problem is accentuated by the lack of a record of interview with Beth's 'secret admirer', a young man who allegedly sat outside her house, day and night and spied on her. The admirer mowed the lawns at her house and showered her with gifts of flowers. Perhaps he was watching her house the night she was murdered. It is understood that in the days after Beth's murder, the admirer had urged another potential witness not to speak with the police.

Another man who was interviewed by police has since said that he knew things about the murder that detectives are still not privy to.

Because the scientific officer, Dr Bentley Atchison, didn't analyse the bloodstained pieces of evidence and the blood specimens taken from the Camerons' house until four weeks after Beth's murder, the police had little knowledge of how much Vivienne Cameron had bled on the night of 22 September. Perhaps if they had known earlier that the not inconsiderable amount of blood in the Camerons' spare bedroom was Vivienne's Type A blood, the focus of their investigation might have been different.

When and why did Vivienne Cameron bleed? According to Fergus Cameron's police statement: 'Vivienne was not injured at all and at no time was she struck'. But Fergus's sister Marnie told detectives she saw blood in the spare bedroom after she came to mind the Cameron children when Vivienne and Fergus went to the Warley Hospital.

Robyn Dixon makes no mention of blood when she came to the Cameron house at 3.20am to pick up the children. At the hospital, when Dr Powles asked Fergus whether the stitches hurt, Fergus said no, while Vivienne said, 'Well you're luckier than I am'. What did she mean?

Perhaps the final word belongs to Rory O'Connor, the first homicide squad detective to attend the murder scene. 'We have these questions that are still unanswered too, but until you talk to Vivienne, there's no way you'll answer a lot of these things,' O'Connor said five years after Beth's murder. 'A lot of these things can't be corroborated – or the person who can corroborate a lot of these things isn't with us... we still haven't found her.'

Epilogue
Where does it end...?

2004

Since writing *The Phillip Island Murder* over a decade ago, I have been contacted regularly by people wanting to know more about the case, people who, like me, let it get under their skin.

Ironically when I first took the story to the publisher in 1991, he told me that the story might suffer because it didn't have a clear ending, but it is the very fact that it didn't have a satisfactory conclusion that it has, over the years, hooked people.

Just before Christmas 2003, Rhonda Byrne from Prime Time Productions contacted me. Her production company has had a lot of interest in their television production on the Easey Street murders called *Sensing Murder*. Capitalising on the public's interest in psychic phenomena made popular by TV psychics like John Edward and Colin Fry, Rhonda's company had two psychics explore the unsolved Collingwood murder of two young women, Susan Bartlett and Suzanne Armstrong in 1977. Hosted by Rebecca Gibney, the show was a ratings winner with an audience of one and a half million viewers. Spurred by its success, and having been given a contract for a further six shows, Rhonda was looking for unsolved Australian crimes and she phoned me. I gave her a brief outline of the Phillip Island case and we chatted about other cases that had entered the Australian psyche – Eloise Worledge, Azaria Chamberlain, the Beaumont children to name but a few.

Because *The Phillip Island Murder* book had gone out of print, I promised to email Rhonda the manuscript to read over the Christmas break. In the email, I typed a warning: *This case will get under your skin too.* And it did.

In real life, crimes are not solved in an Agatha Christie manner where a detective carefully pieces together every scrap of evidence and it's all tied up in the end. Every droplet of blood has its place and reason, and every witness statement matches perfectly. The real world is very different. Some pieces of evidence seemingly have no meaning and others can't be explained away neatly. I understood that when I began researching the Phillip Island case – but my research showed that *too* much didn't make sense. I never set out to write a controversial book – it just happened that way.

It seemed right that Rhonda committed to make a *Sensing Murder* episode on the Phillip Island case because I have always had the feeling that somehow the case wouldn't die because there was something that needed to be straightened out, something that remained unfinished. And the same week that Rhonda originally contacted me, the manager from the popular Prahran crime bookstore, Kill City, phoned me asking if there was any chance of a reprint. She told me that the enquiries for *The Phillip Island Murder* averaged about *two a week!* – this is for a little book that was published in 1993 and went out of print soon after. Someone else told me around this time that some second-hand bookstores near Phillip Island had waiting lists of 50 for second-hand copies of the book. The fanciful might think that this case, which had lain dormant since 1986, was begging for people to take another look. It seems fitting. Nobody has ever been brought to trial for Beth's murder, and Vivienne's disappearance has never been adequately explained.

A couple of months later, Rhonda rang me one afternoon and she was excited. As part of her job, she had to check the details that the psychics gave against the known facts in the murder investigation. In reconstructing the case, she had discovered something that all those years ago, I hadn't noticed, and if the police noticed it, they never told me. Forensic scientist, Dr Bentley Atchison's list of things bloodstained with Type 0, PGM 1 [Beth's blood type] naturally included the doona cover, the pillow case and the bed sheet, but on the list was Item 23: 'the sheets of paper'. Innocuous enough and easy to miss, but Rhonda had made the link. According to Brian Gamble's notes, 'Item 23: two sheets of paper', had been taken from the bed in the Cameron's spare bedroom. Of all the people bleeding that night, Beth was the only one with Type 0, PGM 1 blood, so how did Beth's blood-type get on two sheets of paper found on the Camerons' spare bed when the other blood spots around the spare room were all Type A blood – the same type as Vivienne Cameron?

It could be argued that Vivienne Cameron killed Beth, spattering her blood on the papers and then for some reason drove home with the papers and put them on the spare bed. But there is a problem: Marnie Cairns says clearly in her statement to detectives: 'I had a look around the house and saw blood on the bed in the spare room and also on the bench in the kitchen.' This was when she went back to the Camerons' house to look after the children when Vivienne took Fergus to hospital. Forensic photographs clearly show blood on the papers on the spare bed, as well as on the bedspread, but for some reason, the bedspread is not listed in the evidence later examined by Bentley Atchison. Could that have had Type 0, PGM 1 on it as well?

It seems that the list of questions surrounding the Phillip Island murder of Beth Barnard, and the disappearance of Vivienne Cameron in 1986 grows with each thorough examination. If Vivienne Cameron drove to kill Beth around 3am and Robyn Dixon collected the children shortly after, and told police: 'I saw Vivienne's handbag was on the table inside the back door,' then how did the handbag next appear in the Land Cruiser parked near the bridge? Did Vivienne kill Beth *sans* handbag, and then drive across the Island to her home to get the handbag and then to drive all the way back to the bridge with her handbag only to leave it in the Toyota and then jump from the bridge? Seems unlikely.

Another anomaly: Dianne, Beth's next-door-neighbour, standing on her front porch noticed a car pull into Beth's driveway. *Dianne remembered this car clearly because she had thought it was going to turn into her own driveway. She told O'Connor and Hunter that she had stood outside her house and continued to watch the parked car, with casual interest, because the headlights stayed on for several minutes, before being extinguished. She had wondered why. Because she had been due to go out in 30 minutes, Dianne noted the time was 7.50pm.* And Fergus Cameron says in his statement: 'After I finished work at the penguins about 8pm or shortly afterwards I went to Beth's place...' Did Beth have another visitor that night before Fergus?

If Fergus left the parade not far from his home in Ventnor, and because Beth lived on the other side of the Island, he may not have arrived at her house till 8.15pm. And if the car Dianne saw didn't belong to Fergus, who did Beth know who would park in her driveway for several minutes with the headlights on? In Fergus's police statement, he clearly says: 'I drove up the driveway with my headlights on and parked in the backyard...' He makes no mention of stopping in the driveway for several minutes.

Also interesting was being contacted over the years by people connected with the case who were happy to discuss it after the book was published. I've heard enough rumours to last a life time. It seems in the absence of solid provable truth, people make things up...a friend of a friend saw Vivienne in Wangaratta...people close to Vivienne visit New Zealand – maybe she's there... What I do know for sure is that many on the Island still refuse to discuss the case at all. Even 18 years after it happened!

Another interesting fact came to my attention recently. Vivienne Cameron has two second cousins, Lesley Avery and Pat Hammond. The cousins were researching their family tree and found Vivienne on one of its branches. They went to great lengths to get copies of the Phillip Island book, and developed a great empathy for their newly-discovered cousin. They contacted me and I gave them access to my research. And for them too, the case got under their skin. They frequented the Public Record Office of Victoria and searched out any documentation they could find about Vivienne Cameron. One of the documents they found was Vivienne's Last Will and Testament. Vivienne's handwritten Will was dated 10 June 1984 and it says: *I give to my husband Fergus A S Cameron my estate. If my husband pre-deceases me, I wish my estate to be divided equally between my children. If my husband and children predecease me, I wish my share of the Cameron Agribiz [the family company] to be divided equally between LAD [Donald] Cameron, PG [Pamela] Cameron, ME [Marnie] Cairns, and ID [Ian] Cairns and the remainder of my estate to be divided equally between my brother EKC Candy and my sister DJ Candy.*

When Vivienne's Will was administered, her assets are listed as being worth $190,224.07. In addition to this, Vivienne's step-mother, who had inherited a life-interest in Vivienne's deceased father's house, died recently. Money from the sale of the house was split three ways between Vivienne's sister and brother and Fergus, as Vivienne's heir.

According to *The Age* (25 February 2004), Fergus Cameron spoke of selling the race track to Lindsay Fox. Journalist Stathi Paxinos wrote: 'Placetac managing director Fergus Cameron would not disclose the price for the land, which includes the 106-hectare circuit and 4.4-kilometre track and a permit for a 163-room hotel, but industry sources put the figure at $10 million to $20 million.' Paxinos wrote that Placetac was a 'consortium of Phillip Island landowners'. Close relatives of Vivienne are saddened by the fact that while Vivienne was present for the struggling years on the farm as a young wife and mother, she has missed out on the more lucrative years when the Cameron family business profits have skyrocketed.

So, in 2004, perhaps we should let Sherlock Holmes have the final word: 'It is an old maxim of mine that when you have excluded the impossible, whatever remains, however improbable, must be the truth.'

Vikki Petraitis
2004